ESCHERICHIA COLI INFECTIONS

Second Edition

DEADLY DISEASES AND EPIDEMICS

Anthrax, Second Edition

Antibiotic-Resistant Bacteria

Avian Flu

Botulism, Second Edition

Campylobacteriosis

Cervical Cancer

Chicken Pox

Cholera, Second Edition

Dengue Fever and Other Hemorrhagic Viruses

Diphtheria

Ebola

Encephalitis

Escherichia coli Infections, Second Edition

Gonorrhea

Hantavirus Pulmonary Syndrome

Helicobacter pylori

Hepatitis

Herpes

HIV/AIDS

Infectious Diseases of the Mouth

Infectious Fungi

Influenza, Second Edition

Legionnaires' Disease

Leprosy

Lung Cancer

Lyme Disease

Mad Cow Disease

Malaria, Second Edition

Meningitis, Second Edition

Mononucleosis, Second Edition

Pelvic Inflammatory Disease

Plague, Second Edition

Polio, Second Edition

Prostate Cancer

Rabies

Rocky Mountain Spotted Fever

Rubella and Rubeola

Salmonella

SARS, Second Edition

Smallpox

Staphylococcus aureus Infections

Streptococcus (Group A), Second Edition

Streptococcus (Group B)

Syphilis, Second Edition

Tetanus

Toxic Shock Syndrome

Trypanosomiasis

Tuberculosis

Tularemia

Typhoid Fever

West Nile Virus, Second Edition

Whooping Cough

Yellow Fever

DEADLY DISEASES AND EPIDEMICS

ESCHERICHIA COLI INFECTIONS

Second Edition

Shannon D. Manning, Ph.D.

CONSULTING EDITOR
Hilary Babcock, M.D., M.P.H.,
Infectious Diseases Division,
Washington University School of Medicine,
Medical Director of Occupational Health (Infectious Diseases),
Barnes-Jewish Hospital and St. Louis Children's Hospital

FOREWORD BY
David Heymann
World Health Organization

CHELSEA HOUSE
PUBLISHERS
An imprint of Infobase Publishing

Escherichia coli Infections, Second Edition

Chelsea House
An imprint of Infobase Publishing
132 West 31st Street
New York NY 10001

Library of Congress Cataloging-in-Publication Data

Manning, Shannon D., 1971–
  Escherichia coli infections / Shannon D. Manning ; consulting editor, Hillary Babcock ; foreword by David L. Heymann.—2nd ed.
      p. cm. — (Deadly diseases and epidemics)
  Includes bibliographical references and index.
  ISBN 13: 978-1-60413-253-3 (hardcover : alk. paper)
  ISBN 10: 1-60413-253-1 (hardcover : alk. paper) 1. Escherichia coli infections.
2. Escherichi coli. I. Babcock, Hillary. II. Title. III. Series.

QR82.E6M36 2010
579.3'42—dc22
2010008124

Chelsea House books are available at special discounts when purchased in bulk quantities for businesses, associations, institutions, or sales promotions. Please call our Special Sales Department in New York at (212) 967-8800 or (800) 322-8755.

You can find Chelsea House on the World Wide Web at
http://www.chelseahouse.com

Text design by Terry Mallon
Illustrations by Sholto Ainslie
Cover design by Takeshi Takahashi
Composition by Mary Susan Ryan-Flynn
Cover printed by Bang Printing, Brainerd, MN
Book printed and bound by Bang Printing, Brainerd, MN
Date printed: May 2010
Printed in the United States of America

10 9 8 7 6 5 4 3 2 1

Table of Contents

Foreword 6

1. Outbreaks 8

2. What is *E. coli?* 16

3. *E. coli* Diseases 26

4. *E. coli* Colonization and Transmission 35

5. Epidemiology of *E. coli* Infections 44

6. Disease Pathogenesis 62

7. Diagnosis and Treatment 72

8 Disease Prevention 84

9 Future Possibilities and Concerns 95

Notes 100

Glossary 108

Further Resources 117

Index 125

Foreword

Communicable diseases kill and cause long-term disability. The microbial agents that cause them are dynamic, changeable, and resilient: They are responsible for more than 14 million deaths each year, mainly in developing countries.

Approximately 46 percent of all deaths in the developing world are due to communicable diseases, and almost 90% of these deaths are from AIDS, tuberculosis, malaria, and acute diarrheal and respiratory infections of children. In addition to causing great human suffering, these high-mortality communicable diseases have become major obstacles to economic development. They are a challenge to control either because of the lack of effective vaccines, or because the drugs that are used to treat them are becoming less effective because of antimicrobial drug resistance.

Millions of people, especially those who are poor and living in developing countries, are also at risk from disabling communicable diseases such as polio, leprosy, lymphatic filariasis, and onchocerciasis. In addition to human suffering and permanent disability, these communicable diseases create an economic burden—both on the workforce that handicapped persons are unable to join, and on their families and society, upon which they must often depend for economic support.

Finally, the entire world is at risk of the unexpected communicable diseases, those that are called emerging or re-emerging infections. Infection is often unpredictable because risk factors for transmission are not understood, or because it often results from organisms that cross the species barrier from animals to humans. The cause is often viral, such as Ebola and Marburg hemorrhagic fevers and severe acute respiratory syndrome (SARS). In addition to causing human suffering and death, these infections place health workers at great risk and are costly to economies. Infections such as Bovine Spongiform Encephalopathy (BSE) and the associated new human variant of Creutzfeldt-Jakob disease (vCJD) in Europe, and avian influenza A (H5N1) in Asia, are reminders of the seriousness of emerging and re-emerging infections. In addition, many of these infections have the potential to cause pandemics, which are a constant threat to our economies and public health security.

Science has given us vaccines and anti-infective drugs that have helped keep infectious diseases under control. Nothing demonstrates the effectiveness of vaccines better than the successful eradication of smallpox, the decrease in polio as the eradication program continues, and the decrease in measles when routine immunization programs are supplemented by mass vaccination campaigns.

Likewise, the effectiveness of anti-infective drugs is clearly demonstrated through prolonged life or better health in those infected with viral diseases such as AIDS, parasitic infections such as malaria, and bacterial infections such as tuberculosis and pneumococcal pneumonia.

But current research and development is not filling the pipeline for new anti-infective drugs as rapidly as resistance is developing, nor is vaccine development providing vaccines for some of the most common and lethal communicable diseases. At the same time, providing people with access to existing anti-infective drugs, vaccines, and goods such as condoms or bed nets—necessary for the control of communicable diseases in many developing countries—remains a great challenge.

Education, experimentation, and the discoveries that grow from them are the tools needed to combat high mortality infectious diseases, diseases that cause disability, or emerging and re-emerging infectious diseases. At the same time, partnerships between developing and industrialized countries can overcome many of the challenges of access to goods and technologies. This book may inspire its readers to set out on the path of drug and vaccine development, or on the path to discovering better public health technologies by applying our current understanding of the human genome and those of various infectious agents. Readers may likewise be inspired to help ensure wider access to those protective goods and technologies. Such inspiration, with pragmatic action, will keep us on the winning side of the struggle against communicable diseases.

David L. Heymann
Assistant Director General
Health Security and Environment
Representative of the Director General for Polio Eradication
World Health Organization
Geneva, Switzerland

1

Outbreaks

In early 1982, approximately 47 healthy adults and children living in Oregon and Michigan developed a severe illness with symptoms of stomach pain and cramping followed by episodes of bloody diarrhea.[1] At first, the cause of this disease was a mystery because all of the routine laboratory tests were negative for the known causes of diarrheal illnesses. As a result, no one knew how to treat the sick patients.

*The culprit—a type of bacteria called **Escherichia coli** O157:H7— was ultimately found to be responsible for the outbreak of severe diarrhea.*

The finding that *E. coli* caused the outbreak of diarrheal disease was quite a surprise to health care professionals, because *E. coli* bacteria are very common and generally exist in people's bodies without causing disease. In addition, this newly identified *E. coli* type (O157:H7) was rare and had previously been implicated in only one other case of bloody diarrhea, back in 1975.[2] As a result, a tedious and costly investigation was conducted to determine how these patients acquired this new and rare infection.

By questioning each patient involved in the outbreak, investigators determined that the *E. coli* O157:H7 bacterium was acquired through food—specifically, from raw or undercooked hamburgers purchased at certain McDonald's fast-food restaurants. An inspection of the restaurants revealed that the hamburger meat, or ground beef, was not being cooked thoroughly and therefore, the bacteria was surviving in the meat and was ingested by people.

CONTAMINATED FOOD

After scientists discovered that meat could be the source for a new type of infection, many people immediately wanted to determine who to blame.

DISEASE DETECTIVES

In 1946, the federal government created an agency called the Communicable Disease Center (CDC) in Atlanta, Georgia. The primary role of this agency was to oversee and support state health agencies in the fight against infectious diseases—diseases caused by an agent, such as a virus, bacterium, or parasite. The Epidemic Intelligence Service (EIS), which consists of medical doctors, researchers, and scientists who investigate all types of infectious disease epidemics, was developed in 1951. The creation of this agency enabled the CDC to broaden its scope. EIS officers are often referred to as "disease detectives," because their job is to determine the cause of disease outbreaks, prevent future infections, and help to promote healthy lifestyles. These objectives are critical for maintaining public health.

In 1992, the CDC was renamed the Centers for Disease Control and Prevention, to reflect its role in the prevention of injuries and all diseases, which includes diseases of a noninfectious origin (such as cancer and diabetes) as well. Today, the CDC is still primarily housed in Atlanta, although it has numerous facilities throughout the nation and in other countries.

In 1948, only two years after the creation of the CDC, another important entity—the World Health Organization (WHO)—was created. The mission of the WHO was similar to that of the CDC; however, the WHO monitors disease throughout the entire world. Information exchange among health care officials worldwide has become critical to the understanding of the causes and prevention of diseases.

The CDC Mission

"To collaborate to create the expertise, information, and tools that people and communities need to protect their health—through health promotion, prevention of disease, injury and disability, and preparedness for new health threats."[a]

a. Centers for Disease Control and Prevention. *Mission, 2009*. Available online at *http://www.cdc.gov/od/oc/media/about*.

The public blamed the restaurants, the restaurants blamed the meat supplier, the supplier blamed the meat-processing plant, the plant blamed farmers, and so on. It was unclear who was actually to blame and whether the disease was even significant enough to fight over. After all, the outbreak caused no deaths and only made 47 people ill.

Over the next two years, however, **sporadic**, random, isolated cases continued to be identified and another **outbreak** occurred. This outbreak, also associated with various McDonald's fast-food restaurants in the Midwest, more defintively pointed to ground beef as the source of the infections. The association between *E. coli* O157:H7 infections and hamburgers was confirmed again in January 1993 when the nation's largest *E. coli* outbreak occurred. The source of the outbreak was hamburgers sold at various Jack in the Box fast-food restaurants in Washington, California, Nevada, and Utah. By April 1993, more than 700 people had developed diarrheal disease symptoms, and 56 of them had developed a very severe disease called **hemolytic uremic syndrome (HUS)** after the diarrhea had subsided. In some cases, HUS can cause kidney failure and death, particularly among children. In this 1993 outbreak, HUS cases were identified, and of them four died; all four deaths were in young children.[3]

Food inspection officials later confirmed that the source of the *E. coli* O157:H7 was the Monster Burger, which was part of a promotion and was sold at a reduced price. Demand for the burgers was unusually high, and the restaurant had difficulty keeping up with it. As a result, the burgers were not cooked long enough to kill the *E. coli* bacterium.[4]

Following the chaos associated with the outbreak, most of the victims hired attorneys and numerous lawsuits were filed. Jack in the Box sued the meat suppliers, and, in turn, the suppliers sued their suppliers. The largest personal-injury settlement — in the amount of $15.6 million — went to the family of a nine-year-old girl who was in a coma for 42 days after eating a contaminated hamburger. The girl is reportedly still suffering from injuries as a result of the infection.[5]

DOES *E. COLI* O157:H7 ONLY CONTAMINATE GROUND BEEF?

The 1993 Jack in the Box outbreak led to more strict meat inspection protocols in the United States to ensure that the meat supply was safe for consumption. Most researchers were convinced that *E.coli* O157:H7 contamination was restricted to ground beef and that the bacterium could not survive in other food items. This view changed immediately following the world's largest *E.coli* O157:H7 outbreak to date, which occurred in Sakai City, Japan, in 1996 and affected over 8,000 people, 6,000 of whom were children. The source of the outbreak was contaminated radish sprouts that were included in children's school lunches. This outbreak was the first one associated with fresh produce, which worried health care officials, as the method by which the sprouts became contaminated was not known.

APPLE JUICE AND CIDER

Pasteurization — a technique that is commonly used to treat milk and other beverages — readily kills bacteria that may be present. If a beverage is unpasteurized, however, the chance of contamination increases significantly. Many cases of diarrheal disease have been attributed to the consumption of unpasteurized products. Indeed, *E. coli* O157:H7 outbreaks occurred among people who reportedly drank a specific brand of unpasteurized apple cider in 1993 and 1996. The 1996 apple juice outbreak in the Northwestern states caused diarrheal disease in over 60 people, HUS in 12, and death in a 16-month-old child. These outbreaks confirmed that *E. coli* O157:H7 was not solely linked to ground beef and, therefore, research was required to identify how different food types become contaminated to prevent future outbreaks. Pasteurization is extremely

important because it was determined that the *E. coli* O157:
H7 bacterium can survive for up to 20 days in unpreserved,
refrigerated cider. Consequently, officials recommended more
detailed protocols for cider mill companies involving washing
and brushing apples prior to pressing. Such protocols, however, are not always used and some companies continued to
sell unpasteurized products; therefore, many cider mills have
been forced to shut down.[6]

PETTING FARMS AND ZOOS

In Montgomery County, Pennsylvania, 51 people fell ill with
an *E. coli* O157:H7–associated diarrheal illness that caused
HUS in 15 of the victims. Most of the affected patients were
school-age children. The CDC worked with the Pennsylvania
Health Department to identify the cause of the outbreak. Each
patient was given a survey and asked to answer numerous
questions about his or her behaviors and diet prior to becoming ill. After analyzing the results, investigators identified
a school trip to a specific dairy farm as the contaminating
event; however, the source of the contamination at the farm
was not know. Therefore, investigators used cotton swabs to
take samples of different farm sources, including from the
animals, to assess whether the *E. coli* O157:H7 bacterium
was present.

In addition to finding *E. coli* O157:H7 on a handrail at the
farm, 28 of the 216 cows tested positive; none of the other 43
animal types tested positive. Additionally, the survey results
demonstrated that behaviors promoting hand-to-mouth contact, such as nail biting and eating food before handwashing,
were more common in ill versus healthy individuals who vis-
ited the same farm. Based on this evidence, the investigators
concluded that the cows were the **reservoir**, or source, of the
infectious agent, and that most patients must have acquired
the bacterium by petting the cows. Eating lunch without
handwashing would have given the bacterium access to the
body, thereby initiating the disease process.

Table 1.1 Other notable *E. coli* O157:H7 infections that have been reported to the CDC since 1990[7]

Year	Location	Source of Infection	Number of people affected		
			Diarrhea	HUS	Deaths
1990	North Dakota	Rare roast beef	70	2	0
1994	Montana	Dry-cured salami	20	1	0
1995	Illinois	Swimming in a contaminated lake	12	3	0
1997	Michigan and Virginia	Raw alfalfa sprouts	93	10	0
1998	Alpine, Wyoming	Water	157	4	0
1998	Georgia	Waterpark	26	7	7
1998	Wisconsin	Fresh cheese curds	55	0	1
1999	Washington County Fair, New York	Well water	921	11	2
2000	Washington	Petting zoo	5	1	0
2002	Lane County Fair, Oregon	Sheep and goat	>75	12	0
2002	Cheerleading camp, Washington	Lettuce	>29	1	0
2004	North Carolina	Petting zoo	108	15	0
2006	Multistate	Spinach	204	31	4
2006	Multistate	Lettuce	71	8	0
2007	Multistate	Frozen pizza	21	4	0
2009	Multistate	Cookie dough	69	9	0

Source: Centers for Disease Control and Prevention

Since this initial outbreak in Pennsylvania, numerous additional outbreaks in Florida, Arizona and North Carolina have been associated with farm animals in varying settings that have caused diarrheal disease in more than 170 people.[8] Because of these types of outbreaks, it is now common to see hand sanitizer and handwashing stations at facilities where people may come in contact with farm animals, particularly cows.

WATER

In addition to multiple food items, *E. coli* O157:H7 also survives in water and several outbreaks have been linked to contaminated water used for different purposes. For example, swimming in contaminated lakes, drinking contaminated water at county fairs where farm animals were present, and visiting a waterpark all have been identified as sources of infection.

E. COLI O157:H7 IS HERE TO STAY

Since the initial 1982 outbreak of *E. coli* O157:H7, there have been over 400 additional outbreaks (Table 1.1). As a result, the *E. coli* O157:H7 bacterium has become one of the leading causes of diarrheal disease and foodborne outbreaks in the world. In the United States alone, *E. coli* O157:H7 is responsible for over 73,000 illnesses and 60 deaths each year.[9] In addition, new food vehicles have been identified as important sources of infection. In 2006 and 2007, for example, three *E. coli* O157:H7 outbreaks linked to fresh produce, namely spinach and lettuce, received national attention and had public health officials and consumers extremely concerned about the safety of our food supply. In addition to causing over 360 cases of diarrheal disease, the spinach outbreak, in particular, was associated with much higher rates of HUS than had been observed in previous outbreaks. This finding has led many researchers to hypothesize that a new strain of *E. coli* O157:H7 has emerged that has the ability to cause more severe disease. Indeed, evidence for this hypothesis has recently been documented, as different types of *E. coli* O157:H7 have been found to cause differing frequencies of HUS. It is clear that *E. coli* O157:H7 infections are a major public health concern, and thus, careful monitoring and numerous prevention practices are required to keep these infections under control.

IS *E. COLI* O157 THE ONLY IMPORTANT TYPE OF *E. COLI*?

Although *E. coli* O157:H7 receives the most media attention and is the most widely recognized type of *E. coli* associated with clinical illness in the United States, there are many other types that cause disease. In fact, there are a total of five distinct groups that can cause diarrheal disease or other types of disease: Enterohemorrhagic *E. coli* (EHEC), Enteropathogenic *E. coli* (EPEC), Enteroadherent *E. coli* (EAEC), Enteroinvasive *E. coli* (EIEC), and Enterotoxigenic *E. coli* (ETEC). Not all of the known *E. coli* types are transmitted to people through food or water. Uropathogenic *E. coli* (UPEC), for example, is typically found in a person's intestinal tract and does not always cause urinary tract infections unless the conditions are right and favor bacterial spread to the bladder. In general, knowing which type of *E. coli* is present and causing symptoms is important, as this is how health care providers determine appropriate treatments and how public health officials develop prevention protocols to combat the different types of *E. coli* infections.

2

What Is *E. coli*?

Once we understand the biology of Escherichia coli,
we will understand the biology of an elephant.

—Jacques Monod,
1965 winner of the Nobel Prize
for Physiology or Medicine

Escherichia coli (*E. coli*) is a type of **bacterium**—a tiny singled-celled
organism that can live in many different environments. Bacteria are found in
the soil and water as well as on living organisms, including plants, people, and
animals. In some cases, bacteria are **pathogens** because they cause infections
in people. Many bacteria, however, do not harm people, but rather survive in
people as commensals. In this situation, the bacteria obtain food and benefits
from people without causing symptoms or disease. *E. coli* is typically a commensal, but in specific situations, it can cause a variety of human diseases.

AN IMPORTANT DISCOVERY

E. coli is a **prokaryote**, one of the smallest and most common groups of
organisms in existence. Theodor Escherich, a German **bacteriologist**, or
scientist who studies bacteria, first identified *E. coli* in 1885 in stool specimens collected from babies with enteritis.[1] *Enteritis* refers to an inflammation of the intestine that can cause stomach pain, nausea, vomiting, and
diarrhea in people. To find the bacterium, Escherich had learned the new
technique of culturing, or growing bacteria on petri dishes containing
solidified, nutrient-rich media, from Wilhelm Frobenius, a physician who
had studied bacteriology with Robert Koch.[2] Koch was a bacteriologist
known for creating Koch's postulates, the guidelines used to determine

Figure 2.1 Theodor Escherich, a German bacteriologist who first identified *E. coli* in 1885. (National Library of Medicine)

the infectious agent, or microorganism, responsible for causing a given disease. Because Escherich had learned of Koch's
postulates, he was certain that the agent causing diarrhea in
the babies could be found in their stool samples. By examining

BACTERIA'S FAMILY TREE

Cells are the basic unit of life. They contain important components for an organism's survival and growth. All living organisms are divided into six separate kingdoms based on their physical appearance and structure: Eubacteria, Archaebacteria, Protista, Plantae, Fungae, and Animalia. Each kingdom is separated further by the cellular characteristics of the organisms within them. Most unicellular organisms are part of the Eubacteria (bacteria) and Archaebacteria kingdoms, while organisms from the Plantae (plants), Fungae (fungi), and Animalia (animals) kingdoms are multicellular, or composed of many cells. Bacteria are prokaryotes, whereas the unicellular protists (Protista kingdom) and all other multicellular organisms are eukaryotes. The latter are more complex and are made up of multiple cells that need to work together (Figure 2.2). Each cell has a specific function involved in the organism's growth and survival. In contrast, unicellular organisms contain all the information that they need to live right inside one cell.[a]

After the electron microscope was invented in 1932, scientists could visually observe the differences between bacteria and multicellular organisms. Specifically, in prokaryotes, the genetic material that allows bacteria to survive is free-flowing throughout the cytoplasm, the gel-like liquid inside the cell.[b] In eukaryotes, the genetic material is contained inside a nucleus.

a. The University of Arizona. The Biology Project, 1999. Available online at *http://www.biology.arizona.edu/cell_bio/tutorials/pev/page1.html;* Ramel, G. Earth-Life Web Productions, 2003. Available online at *http://www.earthlife. net/cells.html.*

b. Stanier, R. Y., and C. B. van Niel. "The Main Outlines of Bacterial Classification." *Journal of Bacteriology* 42 (1941): 437–466.

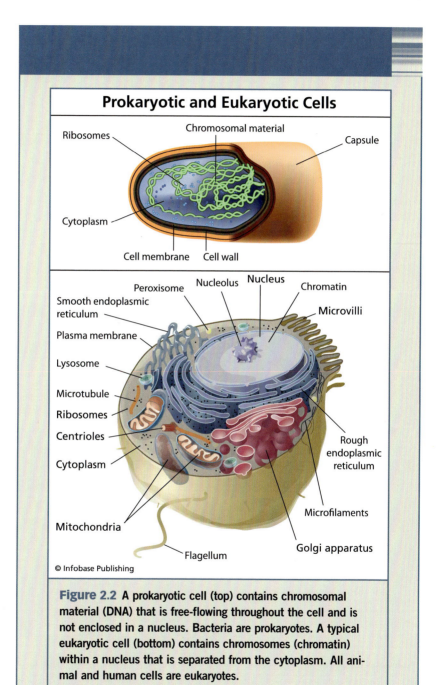

Prokaryotic and Eukaryotic Cells

Ribosomes

Chromosomal material

Capsule

Cytoplasm

Cell membrane   Cell wall

Peroxisome   Nucleolus   Nucleus   Chromatin

Smooth endoplasmic reticulum

Microvilli

Plasma membrane

Lysosome

Microtubule

Ribosomes

Centrioles

Cytoplasm

Rough endoplasmic reticulum

Microfilaments

Mitochondria

Golgi apparatus

Flagellum

© Infobase Publishing

Figure 2.2 A prokaryotic cell (top) contains chromosomal material (DNA) that is free-flowing throughout the cell and is not enclosed in a nucleus. Bacteria are prokaryotes. A typical eukaryotic cell (bottom) contains chromosomes (chromatin) within a nucleus that is separated from the cytoplasm. All animal and human cells are eukaryotes.

their stool samples, he isolated 19 different bacteria with distinct shapes and characteristics, and described a new bacterium that he called *Bacterium coli,* in great detail. These bacteria were shaped like rods (Figure 2.3). The name *Bacterium coli* was later changed to *Escherichia* coli in honor of Escherich.

After characterizing the stool samples, Escherich concluded that the bacteria present in the intestinal tract of babies must be introduced through the environment via direct contact with others as well as the milk they drink.[3] This was a very significant finding at the time because it suggested that humans carry many types of **commensal** bacteria within their bodies that rarely cause disease and therefore, not all bacteria are pathogens. The first *E. coli* strain known to cause diarrhea was not identified until 1935, though detection protocols may have limited the ability to find the bacterium in earlier cases.

THE *E. COLI* FAMILY OF BACTERIA

E. coli belongs to the *Escherichia* genus and is a well-known member of the Enterobacteriaceae family of bacteria. Enterobacteriaceae are commonly referred to as the enteric bacteria, or bacteria that can survive in the **gastrointestinal (GI) tract**, which consists of the digestive system structures (oral cavity, esophagus, stomach, intestines, rectum, and anus). *E. coli* can grow with (aerobically) or without (anaerobically) oxygen or air, an ability that categorizes *E. coli* as a **facultative anaerobe**. Other members of the Enterobacteriaceae family include *Klebsiella, Shigella,* and *Salmonella.* The latter two are commonly associated with **foodborne diseases**, or diseases that are caused by organisms present in food or water. *Klebsiella* bacteria, on the other hand, can cause diseases ranging from urinary tract infections to pneumonia. Both *Klebsiella* and *E. coli* are common commensals, while *Shigella* and *Salmonella* are not.

WHAT'S IN A CELL?

E. coli, like all bacterial cells, carries the information it needs for survival and growth. Inside the cell is a gel-like liquid material

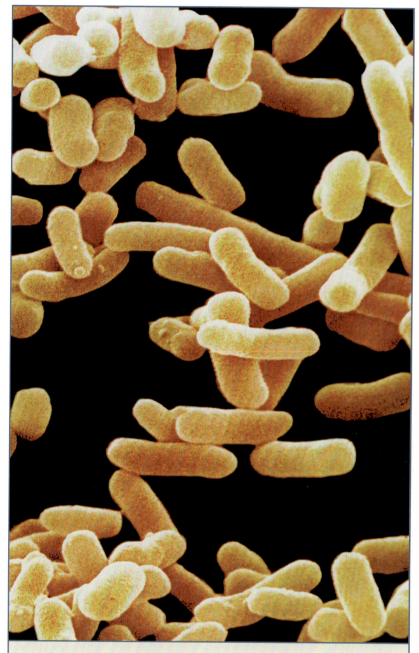

Figure 2.3 *E. coli* visualized by electron microscopy. (©Dr. David Phillips/Visuals Unlimited, Inc.)

THE GRAM STAIN

Bacteria are divided into two groups based on their appearance after a Gram stain test has been performed. Christian Gram developed the Gram stain, a common laboratory technique used today, in 1884. Gram was a young physician from Denmark who noticed that certain bacteria turned violet after staining them with methyl violet dye and an iodine solution, and washing them off with alcohol. He also saw that other bacteria could not be stained in this way. The Gram stain is performed only slightly differently today. Those bacteria that retain the violet stain are considered gram-positive bacteria, whereas those that lose the violet dye and turn red (due to the presence of a counterstain) are called gram-negative (Figure 2.4). The difference in staining is attributed to differences in the composition of the cell wall (Figure 2.5).[a] *E. coli* and all members of the Enterobacteriaceae family are gram-negative bacteria.

a. H. R. Smith and T. Cheasty. "Diarrhoeal Diseases due to *Escherichia coli* and *Aeromonas.*" *Topley and Wilson's Microbiology and Microbial Infections*, eds. L. Collier, A. Balows, and M. Sussman. London: Oxford University Press, 1998.

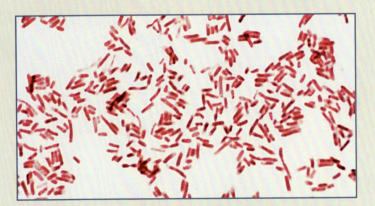

Figure 2.4 This photograph of gram-negative *E. coli* (taken with a light microscope and magnified 400 times) shows the red color of the bacteria when stained using the Gram stain technique. (© Gladden Willis, M.D./Visuals Unlimited, Inc.)

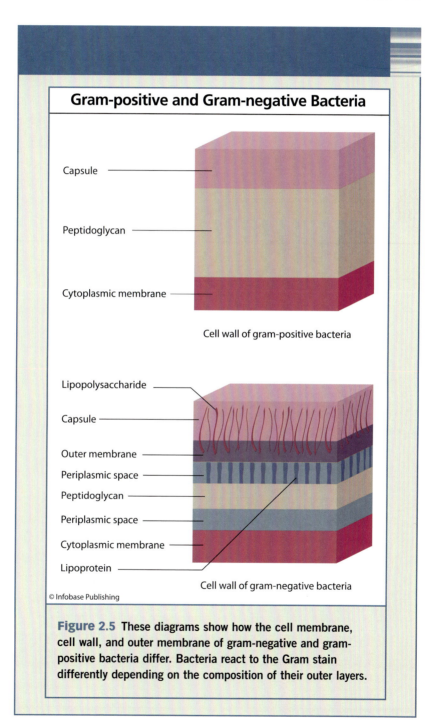

Gram-positive and Gram-negative Bacteria

Capsule

Peptidoglycan

Cytoplasmic membrane

Cell wall of gram-positive bacteria

Lipopolysaccharide

Capsule

Outer membrane

Periplasmic space

Peptidoglycan

Periplasmic space

Cytoplasmic membrane

Lipoprotein

Cell wall of gram-negative bacteria

© Infobase Publishing

Figure 2.5 These diagrams show how the cell membrane, cell wall, and outer membrane of gram-negative and gram-positive bacteria differ. Bacteria react to the Gram stain differently depending on the composition of their outer layers.

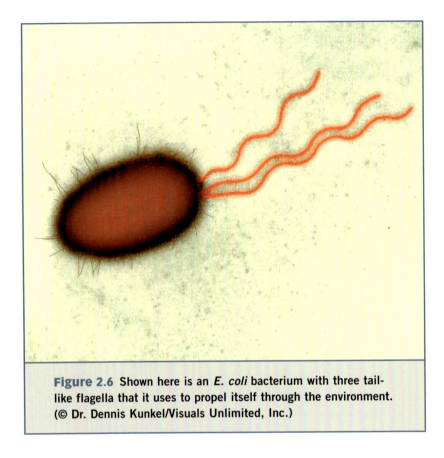

Figure 2.6 Shown here is an *E. coli* bacterium with three tail-like flagella that it uses to propel itself through the environment. (© Dr. Dennis Kunkel/Visuals Unlimited, Inc.)

called the **cytoplasm**, which contains one circular **deoxyribonucleic acid (DNA)** molecule. DNA is a double-stranded molecule that encodes the genetic material unique to every organism.

In bacterial cells, the DNA makes copies of itself in order to reproduce and create a new cell, referred to as a **daughter cell**. This technique is called **cell division**, and it can take place very rapidly under appropriate conditions. In fact, it is estimated that bacteria can divide once every 20 minutes. Daughter cells are initially identical to the original bacterial cell unless a genetic **mutation**—an alteration or change in the genetic material of a cell—takes place during division.

Each bacteria cell contains a thin **cell membrane** that envelops it, surrounded by a very rigid **cell wall** that acts as a protective barrier (Figure 2.2). While the rigidity causes the bacteria to be rather inflexible, it also makes the cell stronger and provides protection from harmful environments. The cell wall consists of two structures: a fluid-filled area called the periplasmic gel that contains a layer of peptidoglycan, and an **outer membrane**. The outer membrane is composed of proteins and fatty acid substances called **phospholipids** and **lipopolysaccharides**. Lipopolysaccharides extend out of the bacterial cell wall and act as **endotoxins**, which are responsible for many of the damaging effects of **gram-negative** bacteria. The outer membrane components work together to enhance bacterial survival and facilitate disease development.

In addition to the outer membrane components, many *E. coli* also have **flagella**, or tail-like appendages that extend from the membrane (Figure 2.6). Flagella are used to propel the bacterium to suitable environments, and are important for bacterial survival.

3

E. coli Diseases

For the most part, diseases are grouped into two distinct categories: infectious or chronic. An **infectious disease** is one that is caused by a micro-organism, such as a bacterium, **virus, parasite,** or **fungus,** whereas **chronic diseases** are conditions that can last for an extended period of time and are generally noninfectious in origin. Some chronic diseases, however, are actually triggered by a pathogen, or infectious agent. Hemolytic uremic syndrome (HUS), which is caused mostly by *E. coli* O157:H7, is an example of a chronic disease that is caused by an infectious agent. HUS typically develops in people weeks after the *E. Coli* O157:H7–mediated diarrhea has subsided and for those individuals who recover, long-term kidney problems are common.

COMMON INFECTIOUS DISEASES

Evidence suggests that infectious diseases have been affecting human populations since before 430 B.C.[1] Today, our society continues to battle infectious diseases, though the types of infections have changed over time. For example, the plague caused by the *Yersinia pestis* bacterium caused the death of up to 24 million people during the 14th century.[2] Smallpox, caused by the variola virus, and syphilis, caused by the *Treponema palli-dum* bacterium, also are considered historical pathogens, since they were first detected in the 14th and 15th centuries, respectively. These days, the plague occurs only rarely, smallpox has been completely eliminated from human populations, and, although syphilis remains a problem in some areas, it is not nearly as common as it once was. Other equally severe infectious diseases, such as diarrheal diseases and influenza, however, have emerged over time to take the place of these illnesses. A new distribution of infectious diseases has resulted.

DIARRHEA: A COMMON INFECTIOUS DISEASE

Among all infectious diseases, **diarrheal disease**, which is characterized by the passage of liquid stools more frequently than is normal for any given person, is a major public health concern. The clinical presentation of **diarrhea** can vary depending on the type of infection. Some people can develop watery, loose stools, while others can have bloody stool. The length of illness also varies considerably. Because of the severe dehydration that follows a prolonged course of diarrhea, it can lead to death in many individuals. Young children are particularly susceptible to diarrheal disease, as are individuals living in developing countries. It was estimated that young children in developing countries can have as many as 10 episodes of diarrhea per year.[3] Although the overall frequency of childhood diarrheal disease is lower in the United States, up to 220,000 children less than five years of age require hospitalization each year because of severe diarrhea.[4] In addition, diarrheal disease has long-term effects on those children who recover from the illness. Some of these effects include decreased growth as a result of reduced appetite, malnutrition, and poor school performance.

In 2004, diarrheal disease was the fifth leading cause of death worldwide contributing to 2 to 3 million deaths per year (Table 3.1). Most of these deaths occurred in children, with 80 percent occurring in the first two years of life. Indeed, among the 10.4 million deaths documented for children under five years of age, diarrheal disease accounted for 16% and ranked second as a leading cause of death in this age group (Figure 3.1). Furthermore, it was estimated that 4 out of 10 of these childhood deaths occurred in Africa.[5]

Diarrheal disease can also present in a more mild form. In the United States, 350 million episodes of mild diarrhea are estimated to occur each year as are 200 million episodes of more severe diarrhea that lasts more than one day and has a major impact on daily activities.[6]

THE ROLE OF POVERTY

The rate of diarrheal disease in developing nations is partly due to the high number of people living in poverty. Recent estimates suggest that approximately 1.5 billion people live

Table 3.1: Top 20 leading causes of death, all ages, 2004

Disease or injury	Death (millions)	Percent of total deaths
1. Ischaemic heart disease	7.2	12.2
2. Cerebrovascular disease	5.7	9.7
3. Lower respiratory infections	4.2	7.1
4. Chronic obstructive pulmonary disease (COPD)	3.0	5.1
5. Diarrheal diseases	2.2	3.7
6. HIV/AIDS	2.0	3.5
7. Tuberculosis	1.5	2.5
8. Trachea, bronchus, lung cancers	1.3	2.3
9. Road traffic accidents	1.3	2.2
10. Prematurity and low birth weight	1.2	2.0
11. Neonatal infections[a]	1.1	1.9
12. Diabetes mellitus	1.1	1.9
13. Hypertensive heart disease	1.0	1.7
14. Malaria	0.9	1.5
15. Birth asphyxia and birth trauma	0.9	1.5
16. Self-inflicted injuries[b]	0.8	1.4
17. Stomach cancer	0.8	1.4
18. Cirrhosis of the liver	0.8	1.3
19. Nephritis and nephrosis	0.7	1.3
20. Colon and rectum cancers	0.6	1.1

a. This category also includes other non-infectious causes arising in the perinatal period, apart from prematurity, low birth weight, birth trauma, and asphyxia. These non-infectious causes are responsible for about 20 percent of deaths shown in this category.

b. Self-inflicted injuries resulting in death can also be referred to as suicides.

Source: World Health Organization, Global Burden of Disease, 2004, http://www.who.int/healthinfo/global_burden_disease/GBD_report_2004update_part2.pdf.

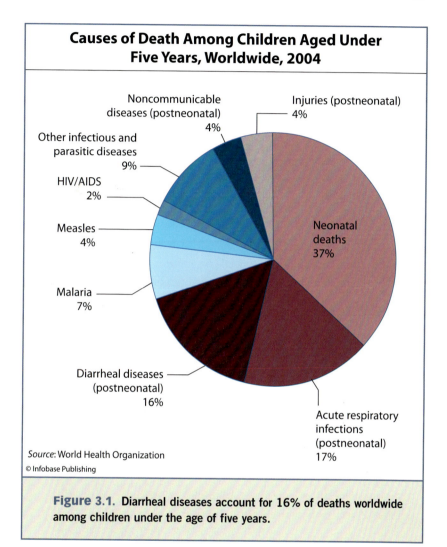

Causes of Death Among Children Aged Under Five Years, Worldwide, 2004

Noncommunicable diseases (postneonatal) 4%

Injuries (postneonatal) 4%

Other infectious and parasitic diseases 9%

HIV/AIDS 2%

Measles 4%

Malaria 7%

Neonatal deaths 37%

Diarrheal diseases (postneonatal) 16%

Acute respiratory infections (postneonatal) 17%

Source: World Health Organization

© Infobase Publishing

Figure 3.1. Diarrheal diseases account for 16% of deaths worldwide among children under the age of five years.

in poverty worldwide and make less than $1.00 a day; this number is continually increasing.[7] Poverty has a tremendous impact on all infectious diseases, since those measures that help halt the spread of disease, including appropriate sanitary conditions, housing, proper maintenance of public water systems and latrines, disease treatment, and important prevention practices, are all costly.

Poverty, however, is not restricted to developed countries. In the United States, for instance, nearly 13% of Americans live below the poverty line. Those Americans most vulnerable to the scourge of infectious diseases are the homeless, who are thought to comprise approximately 1 million people.

E. COLI TYPES THAT CAUSE SEVERE DIARRHEA

More than 20 different kinds of viruses, bacteria, and parasites represent the most common causes of diarrhea. Different types of *E. coli* bacteria, often referred to as **diarrheagenic *E. coli*,** are a leading cause of diarrheal disease in the developing world particularly among children.[8] Among diarrheagenic *E. coli*, enterotoxigenic *E. coli* (ETEC) cause most episodes of diarrhea, which is a major public health concern in at least 13 different developing countries.[9]

The many different *E. coli* types that cause disease in people utilize different mechanisms, thereby contributing to a wide range of symptoms. A complicated naming system is used to distinguish among these diarrheagenic *E. coli* and in most cases, the name reflects the type of disease or the mechanism by which *E. coli* causes disease. For example, *E. coli* O157:H7 is also referred to as **enterohemorrhagic *E. coli*,** (EHEC), because it commonly causes bloody diarrhea. *Entero* comes from the Greek word *enteron*, meaning "intestine," while *hemorrhagic* means "bleeding." Therefore, EHEC is defined as *E. coli* bacteria that cause intestinal bleeding. The other diarrheagenic *E. coli* types include enteropathogenic *E. coli* (EPEC), enteroadherent *E. coli* (EAEC), enteroinvasive *E. coli* (EIEC), and enterotoxigenic *E. coli* (ETEC).

In order to classify the family of diarrheagenic *E. coli* types further, a novel typing method was developed in 1944 that characterizes the type of **polysaccharide** present on the outer surface of the cell (capsule). This is also referred to as the **serotype.**[10] Approximately 173 distinct *E. coli* serotypes exist, ranging from O1 to O173.[11] *E. coli* O157:H7, for example, represents the 157th *E. coli* serotype. The use of serotyping to distinguish between diarrheagenic *E. coli* helps determine whether particular strains are part of an outbreak or are related. Other type-specific characteristics also have been identified and will be discussed in later chapters.

ENTEROHEMORRHAGIC *E. COLI* INFECTIONS

Enterohemmorrhagic *E. coli*, which comprises *E. coli* O157:H7, is known to cause diarrhea; hemorrhagic colitis, or grossly bloody diarrhea preceded by a fever and stomach cramps; and hemolytic uremic syndrome (HUS), a serious long-term complication that primarily affects childrenand can cause kidney failure and death. Adults can present with thrombotic thrombocytopenic purpura (TTP), a severe and often fatal condition similar to HUS.

EHEC are different from other diarrheagenic *E. coli* in that they possess a potent toxin called the **Shiga toxin**. It has been demonstrated that the Shiga toxins released by *E. coli* O157: H7 and other Shiga toxin-producing E. coli (STEC) or differing serotypes damage the vascular endothelial cells—the cells of the tissues that line the internal organs—and facilitate the disease process.

DNA analysis has revealed that there are distinct genetic groupings, or **genotypes**, of EHEC bacteria that have evolved over time and vary in their ability to cause disease. One group includes serotype O157:H7, while another large group is comprised of many different serotypes, including O26:H11, O111: H8 and O118:H16. Genotypes in the latter group have been named non-O157 STEC for simplicity and can cause diarrheal disease in both people and cattle. By contrast, O157:H7 genotypes only cause disease in people, but commonly reside in cattle without causing disease.

ENTEROTOXIGENIC *E. COLI* INFECTIONS

Enterohemmorrhagic *E. coli*, the most predominant type of diarrheagenic *E. coli* worldwide, causes **gastroenteritis**—inflammation of the stomach and intestinal lining that contributes to nausea, diarrhea, stomach pain, and weakness. Gastroenteritis in travelers, called traveler's diarrhea (also referred to as Montezuma's revenge, the GI trots, and Turista), is caused by ETEC bacteria present in the local water or food. The ETEC often differ from the *E. coli* types that people contact regularly at home, and therefore the contact with a new *E. coli* type, combined with the physical stress of traveling, may cause a person to become very sick. In addition to gastroenteritis, traveler's diarrhea can also cause bloating, gas, fever, and dehydration that lasts between three and seven days.[18] Although people who suffer from this condition often feel miserable, traveler's diarrhea is rarely life-threatening in otherwise healthy adults.

In children living in developing countries, however, ETEC infection causes severe diarrhea, particularly in infants who have just been weaned from breastfeeding. It was estimated that roughly 10 to 30% of infants are affected. The transmission of ETEC to infants and children occurs primarily through the food and water in areas with high rates of ETEC-associated disease.[12]

ENTEROPATHOGENIC *E. COLI* INFECTIONS

Enterohemmorrhagic *E. coli*, the first type of *E. coli* identified to cause human disease, attacks the small intestine and causes watery diarrhea that can last for more than 14 days. In developing countries, EPEC is a leading cause of diarrhea in infants and often causes outbreaks within communities. More recently, a new genotype of EPEC has emerged. This genotype is referred to as atypical EPEC and it appears to cause less severe disease than other EPEC types, though the diarrheal symptoms appear to last significantly longer. [13] Atypical EPEC is not restricted to developing countries as was previously suspected. Recent reports suggest that it causes a high frequency of disease in developed countries as well.[14]

ENTEROAGGREGATIVE *E. COLI* INFECTIONS

Enterohemmorrhagic *E. coli* was first identified as a cause of human disease in 1985. In the past, most EAEC infections have occurred in children living in developing countries, however, similar to EHEC and atypical EPEC, EAEC is now considered an emerging pathogen in developed countries. Most people with EAEC infections have watery diarrhea that is sometimes accompanied by blood and mucus. In many cases, the diarrheal episodes are persistent and can last more than 14 days. New studies have found that EAEC can also cause disease in people infected with the human immunodeficiency virus (HIV) as well as travelers.[14]

ENTEROINVASIVE *E. COLI* INFECTIONS

Unlike other diarrheagenic *E. coli*, enteroinvasive *E. coli* tend to more frequently affect children over two years of age, with most illness occurring in children between three and five years. The clinical illness caused by EIEC is quite severe and resembles dysentery or shigellosis, which is caused by specific types of *Shigella* bacteria, a close relative of *E. coli*. Infected individuals can experience fever and abdominal cramping accompanied by either non-bloody or bloody diarrhea. EIEC is considered invasive because it typically invades and destroys those cells lining the colon, thereby causing more severe disease.[15]

NON-DIARRHEAL INFECTIONS CAUSED BY *E. COLI*

In addition to diarrheal disease, *E. coli* also causes a number of other diseases, including meningitis and urinary tract infections (UTIs). A UTI is an infection of the bladder or other structures within the urinary tract. UTIs can develop in both men and women, although they are more common in women. The *E. coli* types that cause UTIs are referred to as **uropathogenic *E. coli* (UPEC)**. Several genotyping studies have demonstrated that UPEC represents a genetically distinct group of strains when compared to diarrheagenic *E. coli* strains. In some people, infection with UPEC can lead to pyelonephritis, a serious illness involving inflammation of the kidneys. Even though pyelonephritis is not as common as UTIs, it is considerably more severe and can lead to death if untreated.

E. *coli* also causes **opportunistic infections**—infections from microorganisms that do not normally cause disease. An example is pneumonia, which can be caused by E. *coli* in individuals with weak immune systems or on ventilators. In general, most people can combat E. *coli* infections via natural immune system defenses; however, some people—particularly children, individuals with existing medical conditions, and the elderly—often cannot ward off an infection without antibiotic treatment. These individuals are more susceptible to illness and long-term complications.

Similarly, newborn babies are extremely vulnerable to all infectious agents, primarily because of their underdeveloped immune system. When infected with E. *coli*, newborns can sometimes develop bacterial sepsis or **meningitis**. Meningitis is a serious condition characterized by inflammation of the meninges, or the membranes that surround the brain. This condition can be fatal and can leave survivors with long-term disabilities, including deafness, blindness, and brain damage. The E. *coli* genotypes that cause newborn meningitis are also genetically different from the diarrheagenic E. *coli* genotypes.

4

E. coli Colonization and Transmission

To cause disease, a pathogen must first be acquired or transmitted to a person. That same pathogen must then be able to survive inside the body, despite having to adapt to a new environment and getting attacked by the human immune system. If successful, the pathogen uses specific structural components to attach to human cells and takes up residence. If the pathogen does not cause disease, then this attachment and residence stage is called **colonization**. For many pathogens, colonization is the first step in the disease process.

E. COLI COLONIZATION IN HUMANS

E. coli bacteria are quite adaptable and can survive in many different environments [e.g., acidic, anaerobic (lacking oxygen) and aerobic (with oxygen)]. In people, *E. coli* most commonly resides in the gastrointestinal tract, where it attaches to mucous membranes, particularly those lining the large intestine (Figure 4.1). Virtually all people are colonized with *E. coli* bacteria, but have no signs of an infection. In other words, they have **asymptomatic colonization** by *E. coli*, which occurs in humans just hours after birth.

Colonization can involve many different types of *E. coli*, which are considered part of the **normal flora**—a group of microorganisms (or microbiota) residing in the body that aid in bodily functions (e.g., digestion) and prevent colonization by pathogenic or harmful microorganisms. The normal flora is constantly changing, with *E. coli* types being lost and

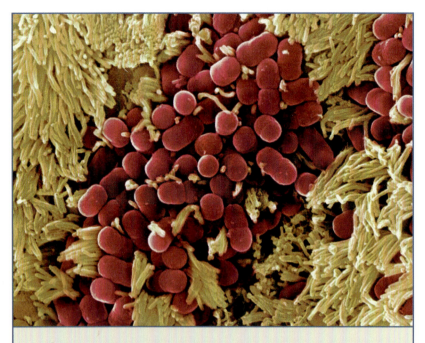

Figure 4.1 *E. coli* adhering to the surface of the small intestine. (© Stephanie Schuller Photo Researchers, Inc.)

acquired regularly via food or direct contact with other people. Many factors including diet, antibiotic use, immune responses, and flora composition, can influence the type and quantity of *E. coli* present in each person.

To cause disease in otherwise healthy people, pathogenic *E. coli* are typically acquired from the environment. In most cases, pathogenic *E. coli* (e.g., diarrheagenic types) do not have the ability to survive for long periods in the body and therefore, rarely colonize humans. By contrast, some potentially pathogenic *E. coli* types (e.g., uropathogenic *E. coli*) commonly colonize humans and are part of the normal flora. In some people, these types can gain access to normally sterile sites such as the urine or blood, thereby causing disease. While variation in the colonization abilities and characteristics of different *E. coli* types plays a critical role in disease development, the human immune response and bacterial density, both of which vary among people, are also important.

E. COLI COLONIZATION IN ANIMALS

Although *E. coli* is present in all mammals as part of the normal flora, some animals are colonized with strain types that can be pathogenic to humans. These animals are considered a reservoir for the pathogen—or the primary environment where the pathogen survives when it is not causing disease in humans. The cow is the main reservoir for *E. coli* O157:H7 and other diarrheagenic *E. coli*; most cattle are colonized in the intestines, yet rectal colonization has also been documented. Pigs and other ruminants, including sheep and goats, are also reservoirs, while other *E. coli* types (e.g., enterotoxigenic *E. coli* [ETEC], enteropathogenic *E. coli* [EPEC]) can reside in both humans and animals.[1] Cattle do not typically develop disease from *E. coli* O157:H7, ETEC or EPEC as humans do, however, they can be colonized with and develop disease from non-O157 EHEC that are capable of producing Shiga toxins. The reasoning behind this variation in infectivity among animals and humans is not clear. It is possible that the genotypes colonizing cattle differ from those that cause human illness, the degree of colonization varies, or that the gastrointestinal tract of cattle differs significantly in its composition, thereby affecting bacterial colonization and disease.

Interestingly, the degree of fecal shedding of *E. coli* in cattle varies by farm and geographic location. For *E. coli* O157:H7, the frequency of shedding ranges between 10% and 100% on any given farm.[2] Young calves also were shown to have the highest level of *E. coli* O157:H7 shedding; however, super-shedders of all ages have been described.[3] Furthermore, shedding is more common in developed versus developing countries, which correlates with the frequency of human disease.

Even though fecal shedding of enterohemorrhagic *E. coli* (EHEC) is an important method for transmitting the bacteria to many animals on one farm, other bacterial sources have been identified, including feeding troughs, commercial feeds, and water troughs. Such sources have been demonstrated to have high levels of EHEC contamination, particularly during the warm summer months.[4]

IMPORTANCE OF LIVESTOCK IN *E. COLI* CONTAMINATION

Because cattle and other animals, particularly sheep, pigs and goats, are frequently colonized with pathogenic *E. coli*, they play a key role in the transmission of these pathogens to humans. Indeed, there are multiple ways in which pathogenic *E. coli* can be acquired by people, but for the most part, these ways typically involve unintentional contact with contaminated animal feces.

As demonstrated by the numerous *E. coli* O157:H7 outbreaks involving the contamination of ground beef, one mode of transmission is foodborne, which occurs by ingesting undercooked, contaminated meat. In fact, it was shown that *E. coli* O157:H7 contamination occurs in 66 of up to 25,000 samples of raw ground beef products.[5] Because the bacterium is often present in cattle at the time of slaughter, the release of intestinal contents containing pathogenic bacteria during carcass prepping can potentially contaminate an entire carcass. For certain meat cuts (e.g., steak), the surface of the meat typically becomes contaminated, while ground meat such as hamburger beef, distributes bacteria throughout the product, thereby making it more difficult to destroy during cooking.

Contaminated water is also an important source of pathogenic *E. coli* on a farm. In fact, it was determined that *E. coli* O157:H7 can survive in water trough sediments for at least six months, even during the winter. When these troughs are emptied, the contaminated water can mix with groundwater and be distributed elsewhere via irrigation systems and taken up by plants and grasses, which are eaten by grazing farm animals and wildlife.[6] *E. coli* contamination of lakes, rivers and streams also occurs regularly, mainly through contaminated runoff from nearby farms.

In addition to exposure to contaminated food and water, direct contact with farm animals, or **zoonotic transmission**, is also important for the transfer of *E. coli* O157:H7 to people. Indeed, several *E. coli* O157:H7 outbreaks have been documented among young children attending petting zoos and farms.

Organic compost, which contains livestock feces and is commonly used as fertilizer, also represents a way in which plants can become contaminated with *E. coli*. If ingested by people, these contaminated plants can cause diarrheal disease. It is not clear whether bacteria are taken up by plants and internalized, or whether they simply exist on the plant surfaces prior to harvesting, processing, and packaging.[7] The fresh spinach implicated in the 2006 multistate *E. coli* O157:H7 outbreak, for example, has been suggested to have only surface contamination that was enhanced through the packaging process, thereby increasing the cell density of the bacterium in the spinach.

DIARRHEAGENIC *E. COLI* TRANMSISSION MODES

Foodborne transmission is the most common mechanism by which people get infected with several types of diarrheagenic *E. coli*. It was estimated that 70–85% percent of ETEC and EHEC cases are the result of foodborne transmission; this percentage is considerably lower (30%) for other diarrheagenic *E. coli*.[8] For *E. coli* O157:H7, many vehicles besides beef and water have been identified including apple juice and cider, salami, lettuce, spinach, sprouts, cheese curd, deer sausage, and raw cookie dough.[9] **Waterborne transmission** also occurs frequently, particularly in regions where sanitary conditions and drinking water are of poor quality. ETEC, for example, can survive in surface waters in endemic regions where it is transmitted to people via bathing, recreation and food preparation. In general, the mode of transmission of both food and waterborne pathogens occurs by the **fecal-oral route,** where fecal-derived bacteria enter a person through their mouth, take up residence in the gastrointestinal tract, and are eliminated in feces.

In addition to foodborne, waterborne, and zoonotic transmission, direct person-to-person transmission also occurs, as many people can become infected with *E. coli* via contact with an infected person. Because *E. coli* O157:H7 has a low **infectious dose** (only 10–100 bacterial cells are required to produce clinical disease) and 1 gram of feces contains 10 million bacteria, it is easily transmitted between individuals, particularly in families.[10] Individuals who acquire the bacterium from another person infected via a different transmission route (e.g., food) are considered secondary infections. The secondary transmission of diarrheagenic *E. coli* to young, more susceptible children in families with other infected members occurs frequently (Figure 4.2). A study of ETEC infections in Bangladesh, for example, found 11% of contacts of infected individuals acquired the infection over a 10-day period and that transmission was associated with socioeconomic status and living conditions.[11] In general, poor hygiene practices and unsanitary conditions both increase the likelihood of secondary transmission, especially among children, who typically wash their hands less frequently than adults. The World Health Organization recently estimated that 1.4 million child deaths from diarrheal disease could be prevented by improving the water supply and its management, sanitary measures and hygiene practices combined with education.

The concept of secondary transmission can be better understood by examining an *E. coli* O157:H7 epidemic curve that plots the number of infections by date (Figure 4.2). The initial peak in an epidemic curve typically represents a point source infection, which highlights the number of individuals exposed to the same, original source (e.g., contaminated food). If the initial peak is followed by another peak, then this can be indicative of secondary infections.[12]

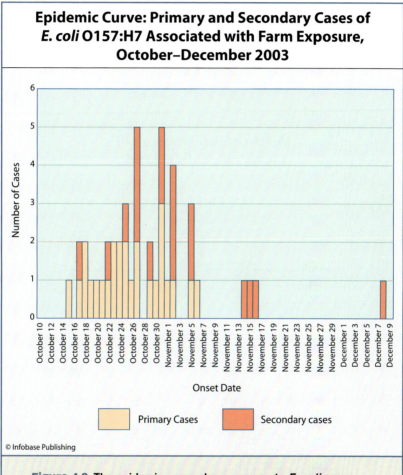

Epidemic Curve: Primary and Secondary Cases of *E. coli* O157:H7 Associated with Farm Exposure, October–December 2003

© Infobase Publishing

Figure 4.2 The epidemic curve above represents *E. coli* cases among a group of Canadian schoolchildren, following exposure to *E. coli* O157:H7 at a petting zoo. Note the initial peak representing the source infection, followed by another peak indicative of secondary infections.[13]

Transmission from one animal, human, or environment to another depends on several interconnected components. Briefly, the transmission cycle for an *E. coli* O157:H7 infection begins with the bovine reservoir, which harbors the bacterium and provides nutrients that facilitate its growth and survival (Figure 4.3). After exiting the bovine reservoir via feces, the bacterium can come into contact with susceptible people via several routes, including food, milk and direct contact. In many cases, secondary transmission of *E. coli* O157: H7 to other people occurs.

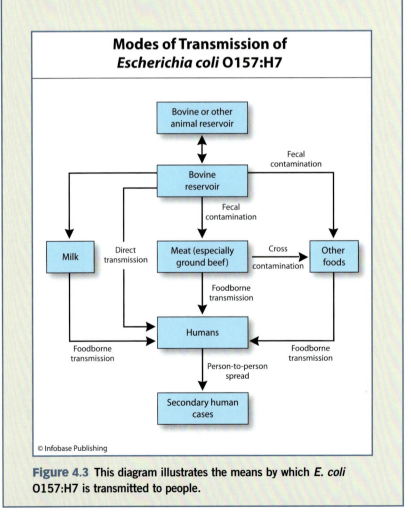

Modes of Transmission of *Escherichia coli* O157:H7

© Infobase Publishing

Figure 4.3 This diagram illustrates the means by which *E. coli* O157:H7 is transmitted to people.

TRANSMISSION OF UROPATHOGENIC *E. COLI*

Uropathogenic *E. coli* (UPEC) resides in the normal flora of genitourinary and gastrointestinal tracts among otherwise healthy individuals. UTIs occur via the mechanical movement of UPEC (e.g., via sexual activity) to the opening of the urethra and up to the bladder where they multiply and cause inflammation (cystitis). In more severe cases, UPEC moves from the bladder to the kidneys to cause pyelonephritis.

Many individuals who develop UPEC-mediated UTIs initially have UPEC in their urine, a medium that is normally sterile, but they do not present with UTI symptoms. This condition is referred to as asymptomatic bacteriuria. Even though individuals with **asymptomatic bacteriuria** do not always develop UTIs, they are capable of transmitting the bacteria to other individuals via sexual contact. Sexual transmission is an important UPEC transmission mode, but like the diarrheagenic *E. coli*, UPEC can also be transmitted by the fecal-oral route.

E. COLI TRANSMISSION TO NEWBORN BABIES

Those *E. coli* types that commonly cause sepsis and meningitis in newborn babies are typically acquired from mothers during the birthing process or through their environment immediately after birth. The mechanism by which mothers and other individuals become colonized is not understood, though foodborne and zoonotic transmission have been suggested to be important. Evidence supporting this comes from studies highlighting the genetic similarities between *E. coli* strains that cause sepsis and *E. coli* strains found in animals and birds.

5

Epidemiology of *E. coli* Infections

Understanding the frequency and distribution of diseases throughout the world is an important first step in eradication. In 1801, Edward Jenner was the first to suggest that infectious diseases could actually be eradicated. At that time, he spoke of "the annihilation of the Small Pox." This implied that humans had the power to eliminate this deadly viral disease, as well as other infectious diseases, permanently. No one knew, however, just how difficult this task would be. After millions of dollars were spent and millions of people were immunized with the smallpox **vaccine**, the disease was finally eradicated from human populations 176 years later.

Disease eradication is often very difficult to achieve for numerous reasons. One example is that changes in the pathogen and/or changes in the pathogen's location relative to human populations can stifle control efforts. Despite this, eradication remains an important goal of health care organizations worldwide. To date, smallpox eradication has been the only completely successful program, in that the disease no longer exists outside of laboratories.

Failed eradication programs have illustrated to scientists that it is essential to fully understand how the targeted disease affects humans and in what capacity. For example, gaining a better understanding of the causative agent, its transmission dynamics and life cycle, and its mechanism of survival in humans is necessary to assess whether eradication efforts are feasible. Additionally, it is imperative to understand the distribution of the disease on a global scale. All of these topics fall under the discipline of **epidemiology**—the study of the occurrence, distribution, transmission, and prevention of disease in specific populations. **Epidemiologists**, individuals who study epidemiology, play a key role in enhancing our understanding of the disease process and identifying people who may be more susceptible to developing certain infections.

HISTORY OF EPIDEMIOLOGY

The Greek physician Hippocrates, considered the founder of human medicine, suggested in the fifth century B.C. that human disease is the result not only of one's internal environment, but also of one's external environment. This observation suggests that numerous factors work together to cause human disease. These risk factors may be related to the environment, the affected person (host), or the causative agent (pathogen). Examples of environmental factors include climate, land design, and sanitation practices, while factors specific to the host may include age, gender, nutritional status, and the type of immune response elicited. Factors specific to the pathogen may include particular components produced by the agent, such as the Shiga toxin produced by *E. coli* O157:H7, which facilitates kidney disease development. In most cases, all of these factors work together to cause disease, though for any given disease some factors may be more important than others.

In addition, a British merchant named John Graunt made the first attempt to quantify disease patterns in a population in 1662. By researching the birth and death rates of people living in London, Graunt collected data that specifically provided information about human diseases. However, the most famous historical epidemiologist was a British physician named John Snow, who identified the link beteween cholera and diarrheal disease associated with contaminated drinking water from a specific pump in London.

A common way that epidemiologists assess the distribution of specific diseases in a population and are alerted to the arrival of an emerging pathogen is by developing a **surveillance system**. These systems rely on the interactions of numerous people and institutions (e.g., health care providers, clinical laboratories, public health officials, hospitals, and the public), located in distinct geographic areas, to watch for and report disease information back to the epidemiologists. Data generated from surveillance systems allow epidemiologists to measure disease frequencies, monitor trends, make comparisons between geographic locations, and identify people and areas that are more prone to the development of the disease.

There are several types of surveillance systems that are used by epidemiologists. One example is an active surveillance system—or a system in which surveillance personnel actively contact clinical laboratories to obtain data. By contrast, a passive surveillance system relies on clinical laboratories to report data; passive systems are typically less reliable than active systems.

FOODBORNE DISEASE SURVEILLANCE IN THE UNITED STATES

In 1996, the CDC created an active population-based surveillance system to detect illnesses and monitor disease trends caused by the most common foodborne pathogens. The name of the system is FoodNet and it was first set up to identify seven different types of bacterial pathogens, including *Campylobacter, Listeria, Salmonella*, STEC O157, *Shigella, Vibrio*, and *Yersinia*. Since its inception, FoodNet has added two parasites (*Cryptosporidium* and *Cyclospora*) as well as non-O157 STEC, and it now collects information on outbreaks caused by each of these pathogens. Other diarrheagenic *E. coli* (e.g., ETEC, EPEC, EAEC, EIEC) are not monitored by FoodNet, as the incidence in the United States is quite low relative to the other pathogens. FoodNet utilizes surveillance data generated in 10 different states located in distinct geographic locations around

HEALTHY PEOPLE 2010

In 2000, the United States Department of Health and Human Services in collaboration with the CDC developed Healthy People 2010, a plan that involves promoting health and preventing disease (http://www.cdc.gov/nchs/about/otheract/hpdata2010/abouthp.htm). There are currently 467 objectives that act as guidelines to improve the health of people living in the United States. The main goals of Healthy People 2010 are to increase individual quality of life and eliminate health disparities. All 467 objectives make up 28 focus areas and food safety is one of them. Food safety is clearly important, as 76 million people get sick each year from foodborne illness, contributing to 300,000 hospitalizations and 5,000 deaths and yielding annual costs of $23 billion. Food safety guidelines established through Healthy People 2010 aim to prevent foodborne infections by creating disease frequency targets over time. One example is *E. coli* O157:H7, as the 2010 target for incidence of infection is 1.0 cases per 100,000 people; according to data from 2007, this target has not yet been met.[1]

the United States. These sites correspond to 15% of the nation's population (45.5 million people), and is relatively representative with the exception of a slight underrepresentation of the Hispanic population.[2] Each site obtains detailed epidemiological data from patients such as age, gender, date of onset, symptoms, hospitalization, and recent food and travel history, as well as molecular data for each pathogen.

In 2007, a total of 17,883 cases of infection with common foodborne pathogens were identified via FoodNet. To calculate the incidence, the total number of laboratory-confirmed infections caused by each pathogen was divided by the total number

MEASURING DISEASE FREQUENCIES

The most basic measure of disease frequency is a count of the number of affected people at a single point in time. It is also important to know the size of the population at risk, or that could potentially be affected, and identify a specific period of time to be evaluated. The prevalence, calculated as the number of infected people divided by the total number of people in a given population, is a very important measure of disease frequency. To determine whether a specific disease is increasing in frequency in a particular area, epidemiologists must be aware of the endemic disease level—or the background frequency level of disease that is usually present in a given population. If the number of disease cases increases rapidly and significantly above the endemic level, then the situation is referred to as an epidemic or outbreak. A specific outbreak that occurs in multiple countries at the same time is called a pandemic. Another important measure of disease frequency is the incidence, or number of new infections in a given population during a specific time period. This differs from the prevalence in that it measures only new cases in an area and does not count people who have already had a given disease for a long period of time. For the most part, the incidence and prevalence vary by geographic location, population type and size, and pathogen.

of people in the surveyed population. *Salmonella* infections were observed most frequently (n=6,790; incidence=14.92) followed by *Campylobacter* (5,818; 12.79), *Shigella* (2,848; 6.26), *Cryptosporidium* (1,216; 2.67), STEC O157 (545; 1.20), STEC non-O157 (260; 0.57), *Yersinia* (163; 0.36), *Listeria* (122; 0.27), *Vibrio* (108; 0.24), and *Cyclospora* (13; 0.03) in 2007. Differences in the distribution of these pathogens, however, varied among surveillance sites (Figure 5.1), which may be due to true geographic differences or variation in the ability to identify cases. The incidence per 100,000 for children under five years of age was highest for infections caused by *Salmonella* (62.11), *Shigella* (27.77), *Campylobacter* (24.01), and STEC O157 (3.66).[3]

FOODBORNE DISEASE OUTBREAKS IN THE UNITED STATES

In addition to FoodNet, the CDC also has been monitoring foodborne disease outbreaks since 1966. Unlike FoodNet, this is a passive surveillance system that has relied on reporting from participating laboratories around the nation. In recent years, however, the CDC has increased communication with laboratories and in 2001, a Web-based outbreak reporting form was established, thereby increasing the reliability of the system.

Between 1998 and 2002, 6,647 foodborne disease outbreaks were reported, with an average of 1,329 outbreaks per year. The cause was only known for 2,167 (33%) of the reported outbreaks, accounting for 54% of all 128,370 illnesses. Among the outbreaks with a known cause, bacterial pathogens were most commonly implicated (55%) followed by viruses (33%), chemical agents (10%), and parasites (1%). Diarrheagenic *E. coli* contributed to 140 outbreaks affecting 4,854 people and causing 4 deaths during the 5-year period. EHEC, ETEC, and EAEC caused 132, 7 and 1 outbreaks, respectively, of the 140 outbreaks attributable to diarrheagenic *E. coli*. The majority or *E. coli* outbreaks (58%) involved food prepared at home (*n*=40), restaurants (*n*=41), schools (*n*=9), picnics (*n*=7), camps (*n*=6), churches (*n*=5), cafeterias (*n*=2), daycare centers (*n*=2), and other locations (*n*=45).[4]

TRACKING FOODBORNE OUTBREAKS

After a foodborne bacterial pathogen is identified in a patient, public health laboratories characterize it using a variety of

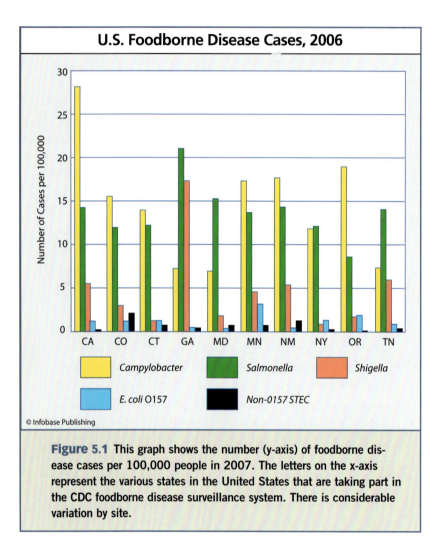

Figure 5.1 This graph shows the number (y-axis) of foodborne disease cases per 100,000 people in 2007. The letters on the x-axis represent the various states in the United States that are taking part in the CDC foodborne disease surveillance system. There is considerable variation by site.

molecular methods. One of the most important methods is **pulsed-field gel electrophoresis (PFGE),** which essentially provides a DNA fingerprint of each pathogen and is used to assess whether strains differ at the genetic level. Briefly, DNA is isolated and combined with a **restriction enzyme**, or a digestive enzyme that cuts the DNA into fragments at specific restriction sites. An electric current then sorts the DNA fragments by size and density, with the smaller, less dense fragments moving the fastest and migrating the farthest down the gel. The end result is a banding pattern that contains many lines, or DNA fragments, of varying sizes. Each genetically distinct strain will have a unique banding pattern, which is dependent on the number and location of restriction sites in a given genome.

The use of PFGE is especially important during an outbreak. Bacterial strains isolated from different patients with identical PFGE banding patterns are initially considered to have originated from the same source unless epidemiological data demonstrate otherwise. In a typical outbreak situation, different people with similar exposures may be infected with strains of the same PFGE pattern. For example, the source of the 1993 EHEC O157:H7 Jack in the Box outbreak was identified because the EHEC strains from the hamburgers and patients were identical by PFGE.

In 1996, the CDC created PulseNet, a network of public health laboratories that utilize PFGE to examine foodborne bacteria, including *Shigella*, *Salmonella*, EHEC O157:H7, *Listeria monocytogenes*, and *Campylobacter*. The primary purpose of PulseNet is to serve as an early warning system to detect outbreaks and, since its inception it has been instrumental in the detection of numerous foodborne outbreaks. After PFGE is completed on suspect bacterial strains, the banding patterns are imported into an electronic database that is shared with other laboratories in an effort to identify other strains with identical patterns (Figure 5.2). The identification of a particular banding pattern in multiple locations during a short period of time is often indicative of an outbreak. This rapid-detection system provides more time for public health officials to determine the source in order to prevent additional disease cases.

ENTEROHEMORRHAGIC *E. COLI* INFECTIONS

Although the FoodNet system tracks both *E. coli* O157:H7 and non-O157 enterohemorrhagic (EHEC) infections, the reported frequencies may actually underestimate the true frequencies.

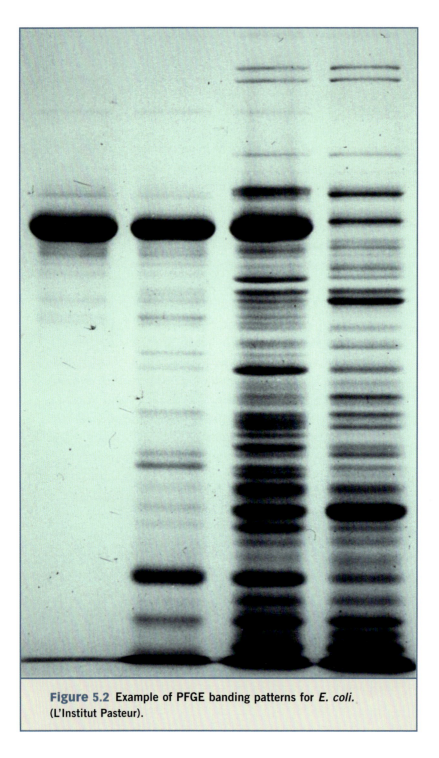

Figure 5.2 Example of PFGE banding patterns for *E. coli*. (L'Institut Pasteur).

This underestimate is due to the inability of some clinical laboratories to detect the pathogens, variation in case reporting and **case definitions**, and the fact that not all ill individuals will seek medical care or provide a stool specimen for evaluation.

Although the incidence of *E. coli* O157:H7 was estimated to be 1.20 per 100,000 cases in 2006 in the United States, this incidence rate has varied over time. When compared to the period between 1996 and 1998, for example, the number of infections caused by *E. coli* O157:H7 in 2007 had decreased by 25%. A similar decline in incidence was observed between 2004 and 2005, though this decline has not been maintained to date.[5] It also has been shown that *E. coli* O157:H7 infections occur more frequently in the warm summer months when the likelihood of food contamination is higher (e.g., at picnics; Figure 5.3).

Epidemiological studies have demonstrated that non-O157 EHEC infections occur just as frequently as *E. coli* O157:H7 in the United States, but they are even more common in other parts of the world, including Argentina, Australia, and Germany.[6] In Germany, for instance, non–O157 EHEC causes 80% of the diarrheal illnesses attributable to all EHEC infections.[7] Belgium, Finland, the Czech Republic, and Italy also have observed higher rates of non-O157 EHEC when compared to *E. coli* O157:H7.[8] Interestingly, the *E. coli* O157 infections that occur in Germany are typically caused by genetically distinct strain types (O157:H-negative) than those found in the United States; these distinct types are also capable of causing severe disease and large-scale outbreaks of HUS in children. [9]

The primary risk factor for EHEC infection is consumption of feces-contaminated food, as 80% of *E. coli* O157:H7 and non-O157 EHEC cases were found to result from foodborne transmission.[10] Interestingly, only 86 (15.8%) of the *E. coli* O157:H7 infections identified in 2007 were associated with outbreaks indicating that the majority of EHEC cases are sporadic.[11] Despite this, *E. coli* O157:H7 still causes 17 outbreaks per year in the United States. [12] It was estimated that 350 *E. coli* O157:H7 outbreaks occurred between 1982 and 2002 in the

United States, which affected 8,598 people, with 1,493 (17%) of these individuals requiring hospitalization, 354 (4%) developing HUS, and 40 (0.5%) dying as a result of the infection. [13]

The epidemiology of *E. coli* O157 infection has changed dramatically since it was first identified in the early 1980s, with new infection sources (e.g., raw cookie dough) being identified regularly.[14] These changes are likely influenced by the genetic variation and evolution of the EHEC O157 pathogen population, as emergent strain types acquire novel factors that contribute to disease pathogenesis and outbreaks.[15]

HEMOLYTIC UREMIC SYNDROME

Surveillance for patients with hemolytic uremic syndrome (HUS) was recently incorporated into FoodNet. To identify HUS cases in FoodNet surveillance sites, the CDC uses a complex network of pediatric nephrologists, or kidney specialists, as well as infection control practitioners. A standard case definition is used for categorizing HUS cases; however, there are concerns that this definition is not stringent enough and can contribute to **misclassification bias**. Nevertheless, monitoring the frequency of cases that develop more severe disease is extremely important to fully understand the disease burden attributable to EHEC infections.

In 2006, a total of 82 HUS cases were identified via FoodNet, with 58 (0.7%) occurring in children less that five years of age. The incidence per 100,000 was 0.78 for children under 18 years of age and 2.01 for children less than five years. Because *E. coli* O157:H7 is the most common cause of HUS in the United States, it is not surprising that the frequency of HUS mimics that of *E. coli* O157:H7. Other countries, however, have varying HUS rates. Argentina, for example, has the highest rate of HUS worldwide affecting 12.2 per 100,000 children less than five years of age; the majority of these cases are caused by non-O157 EHEC.[16] Australia, Germany and Austria also observe higher frequencies of HUS caused by non-O157 EHEC than *E. coli* O157:H7.[17]

Several HUS risk factors have been identified including African descent, living in a rural area, season, and geography.[18] These factors, however, are not consistently significant in different populations, which could be due to variable detection protocols and HUS case definitions, or may actually represent real risk differences by population. It is important to note that the risk of developing HUS is directly linked to the risk of O157 infection, as the same behaviors that contribute to O157 infection (e.g, consumption of undercooked meat, animal contact, etc.) also put an individual at risk for developing HUS.[19] This explains why HUS disease rates have paralleled *E. coli* O157:H7 infection rates

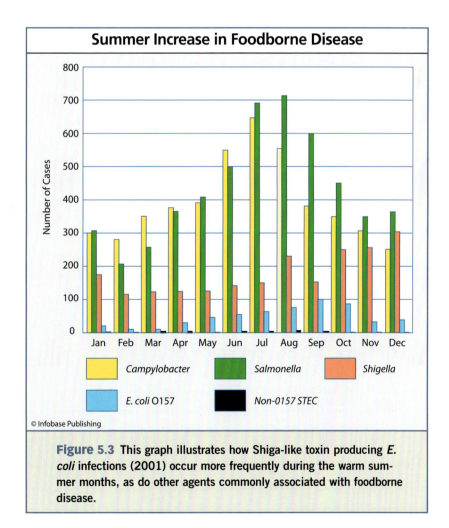

Figure 5.3 This graph illustrates how Shiga-like toxin producing *E. coli* infections (2001) occur more frequently during the warm summer months, as do other agents commonly associated with foodborne disease.

over time.[20] In general, risk factors for HUS are poorly understood, as large-scale epidemiological studies using set definitions
and protocols have not been conducted to date. Such studies are
extremely important given the significant morbidity and mortality associated with HUS in young children as well as the high cost
($39,000–$7,000,000 per case) to society.[21]

ENTEROPATHOGENIC *E. COLI* INFECTIONS

Determining the prevalence and incidence of enteropathogenic *E.
coli* (EPEC) infections is somewhat difficult, as the frequency has
been shown to vary by study population and age group. Differences in detection methods and case definitions also pose a problem; however, this is true for all diarrheagenic *E. coli*. Despite this,
EPEC remains an important diarrheal disease pathogen affecting
5% to 20% of children less than two years of age in developing
nations.[22] Unlike other diarrheagenic *E. coli*, however, older children also commonly develop EPEC infections. A study in Tunisia,
for instance, found the highest prevalence of EPEC infection in
children between 6 and 12 years of age (20%) followed by children
less than two years of age (15%).[23]

Recent studies have demonstrated that the prevalence of
EPEC infections has increased in developed nations, though
these infections are caused primarily by atypical EPEC, an
emergent genotype that is distinct from typical EPEC. For
example, 22% and 43% of diarrheal infections in Norway
and Australia, respectively, were caused by atypical EPEC.[24]
Another study of diarrhea in 32 Mexican children less than
two years of age identified atypical EPEC in 41%, whereas
typical EPEC was found in only in 9%.[25]

Similar to EHEC, EPEC infections tend to occur in warm
and humid weather. In Mexico, for example, the frequency
of EPEC infections has been reported to increase during the
rainy season (May through June) where water contamination
is more common. Several studies have also demonstrated that
children and adults without symptomatic infections can have

EPEC. A study of children with and without diarrhea in Tunisia detected typical EPEC in 11% of children without diarrhea; ETEC, EHEC, and EAEC also were found demonstrating that these potential pathogens can also be part of the normal flora of some people.[26]

ENTEROTOXIGENIC *E. COLI* INFECTIONS

For the most part, enterotoxigenic *E. coli* (ETEC) represents the most common type of diarrheagenic *E. coli* in developing countries where the pathogen is endemic. Young children living in endemic regions are more likely than adults to become infected with ETEC and develop severe illness because immunity has been shown to increase with age. Several studies have demonstrated that ETEC more frequently attacks infants less than two years of age as well as males more than females.[27] In Mexico, for example, ETEC was reported to cause diarrhea in 37.5% of 32 children less than two years of age.[28] Additionally, an Egyptian study of 211 newborn babies demonstrated that the median time to develop an ETEC infection was eight months of age.[29]

Among a recent evaluation of 51 published studies of travelers' diarrhea, ETEC caused 1,678 infections, which affected 30% of the population (*n*=5,518) studied. The highest rates of ETEC disease were observed in Latin America and the Caribbean, Africa, South Asia, and Southeast Asia. In these endemic areas, most ETEC infections occur during the wet summer months as well as rainy seasons in regions with concomitant periods of heavy rainfall. Warm temperatures facilitate bacterial growth in the environment and heavy rains contribute to contamination of surface waters with fecal material.[30] Among travelers, however, infection can occur during any time or season. It was estimated that 20 to 60% of travelers will develop diarrheal disease from exposure to ETEC via food or water, and travelers from developed versus developing countries are more commonly affected.[31]

ENTEROADHERENT AND ENTEROINVASIVE
E. COLI INFECTIONS

Both enteroadherent *E. coli* (EAEC) and enteroinvasive *E. coli* (EIEC) infections occur more frequently in developing versus developed countries. In an analysis of published studies, EAEC caused diarrheal disease in a median of 15% of children in developing countries and 4% of children in developed countries, and was observed most frequently in Latin America (24.1%), South Asia (16%).[32] An unusually high prevalence of EAEC was observed in Brazil affecting 68% of the 56 children studied, while no infections were attributable to EAEC in a Mexican study of 32 children younger than two years of age.[33] EIEC, on the other hand, typically occurs in less than 4% of individuals with diarrheal disease, though a recent study in Ecuador identified it as the leading cause of diarrheal disease (3.2 cases for 100 people), particularly in children under the age of five.[34] These data demonstrate that there is considerable variation in the prevalence of both pathogens by geographic location. The reason for this variation is not known, however, differing detection protocols may play a role.

Despite the lower frequency of EAEC and EIEC infections in developed countries, both pathogens have caused a few notable foodborne outbreaks, and the prevalence of EAEC appears to be increasing worldwide.[35] EAEC, for example, was present in 19 (10.2%) of 187 children with diarrhea and three (2.2%) of 137 children without diarrhea in Switzerland; most children were under five years of age.[36] EAEC also has caused large-scale diarrheal disease outbreaks in the United Kingdom, France, Switzerland, and Japan.[37] In the United States, EIEC has been implicated in outbreaks associated with contaminated cheese and guacamole, which affected 226 and 370 people, respectively.[38] In addition to exposure to contaminated food or water and travel to endemic regions, few risk factors have been identified for both EAEC and EIEC infections.

DIFFUSE ADHERING *E. COLI* INFECTIONS

Diffuse adhering *E. coli* (DAEC) was first identified by its unique adherence pattern in the laboratory; two classes of DAEC strains are common, with one causing mostly UTIs and the other causing more typical diarrheal infections. Similar to EAEC, many DAEC strains are nonpathogenic. This, however, is dependent on the patient population, as prior studies have detected DAEC in young children more frequently than babies, for example.[39]

Few epidemiological studies have been conducted to determine the prevalence of DAEC in different poplulations, which may be due to difficulties associated with detection. As with other diarrheagenic *E. coli*, there appears to be considerable geographic variation. A Brazilian study, for example, identified DAEC to be the most prevalent *E. coli* type in children over the age of one year and in individuals reporting diarrheal illness, while an African study found DAEC to be the second most common pathogen in children under two years behind EAEC.[40]

UROPATHOGENIC *E. COLI* INFECTIONS

The epidemiology of uropathogenic *E. coli* (UPEC)-mediated urinary tract infections (UTIs) has been studied extensively, primarily because of the magnitude of the problem. It was estimated that UPEC affects 150 million people each year and causes 70–90% of community-acquired UTIs and 40 percent of **nosocomial** UTIs—or those infections that are acquired in a hospital or health care environment.[41] Because of anatomical differences, women in every age group have a higher annual incidence of UTI than men (12.6% compared to 3.0%) and often have recurrent infections. Over half of all women will have at least one UTI by the age of 32, while only 20% of men in their seventies have reported having a UTI.[42] This risk of more severe disease, which requires hospitalization, is also higher in women. Hospitalization rates for pyelonephritis are 11 per 10,000 women and only 3 per 10,000 men; pregnant women are often more likely to be hospitalized than nonpregnant women as are diabetic men and women.[43] Men, however, have been shown to have higher mortality rates (16.5 per 1,000) during hospitalization than women (7.3 per 1,000); these rates increase with age, number of procedures, and diagnoses.[44]

Numerous risk factors are associated with UTIs, including type and frequency of sexual activity, use of condoms, spermicides, diaphragms, or urinary catheters, recent antibiotic use, and diabetes. Anatomical problems such as an inability to fully empty the bladder, obstructed urine flow, and bladder trauma, also put an individual at higher risk for UTIs, while drinking cranberry juice was shown to be protective.[45] Few risk factors have been identified for pyelonephritis, though the genotype of the UPEC strains is extremely important, as these strains represent a genetically distinct subset of UTI strains.

The total costs associated with treating UTIs in otherwise healthy women, who do not require hospitalization, were estimated to be $1.6 billion in the United States in 1995. These costs are likely to be much higher in the present. For nosocomial UTIs, treatment requires on average, one extra day of hospitalization that results in nearly 1 million extra days of hospitalization and a total cost of up to $451 million each year.[46]

SEVERE *E. COLI* INFECTIONS IN BABIES

Few epidemiological studies have been conducted to calculate the incidence of and identify risk factors for early-onset (<7 days old) *E. coli* bloodstream infections (sepsis) in newborn babies. It has been estimated that 0.3 babies per 1,000 live births develop *E. coli* sepsis each year, but the rate appears to be higher in some populations and is thought to be increasing, particularly among babies with very low birth weights.[47] In a study of 408 early-onset sepsis cases identified in California and Georgia between 1998 and 2000, 70 (17.2%) had infections caused by *E. coli,* and most of these babies were premature.[48] In the same study, an increase was observed in the frequency of antibiotic resistant *E. coli,* or *E. coli* strains that are resistant to an antibiotic's killing mechanism, and death was more common in babies with resistant infections.[49]

Risk factors thought to be important for *E coli* sepsis include exposure to antibiotics during childbirth, prematurity (gestational age <33 weeks), maternal fever during childbirth, and prolonged period between placental membrane rupture and delivery were associated with increased risk.[50] Antibiotic exposure is particularly important for the development of resistant infections.

6

Disease Pathogenesis

Microorganisms contribute to disease via complex pathways that depend on multiple interactions. **Pathogenesis**, the development of disease, occurs as a result of the interactions between the host, pathogen, and environment. Exposure to a specific pathogen is not enough to cause disease in some individuals, though it is necessary. For diarrheagenic *E. coli*, specific environments (e.g., food, water, farm animals) are more likely to harbor the pathogens, while certain people exposed to a pathogen in a given environment are more susceptible to developing infections (e.g., babies, the poor and malnourished, diabetics, individuals with weak immune systems). In addition, the bacterium, which contains a repertoire of **virulence factors** (features that are encoded by **virulence genes**) important for establishing a niche or causing disease in a host, is a critical component for disease.

In order for disease to develop in any individual, an infectious agent must be able to gain entry, colonize and proliferate in the host. This is not a simple task, since the human body is equipped with immune cells, acidic environments, and is crowded with millions of commensal microorganisms (normal flora). Most infectious agents, however, have developed strategies that increase their ability to survive in such an environment.

MECHANISMS OF *E. COLI* INFECTION

All *E. coli* types have similar infection strategies: (1) entry and travel through the body; (2) colonizing mucosal surfaces; (3) avoiding clearance by immune cells; (4) proliferating; and (5) causing damage to the host.[1]

The first step in the disease process is to gain entry to the body and travel to a potential colonization site. Diarrheagenic *E. coli* gain entry via

BACTERIAL VIRULENCE

The capacity of a bacterium to cause disease (its virulence) is measured by the severity of the resulting disease. For instance, infections caused by EHEC are typically more severe than ETEC infections. The difference in the clinical presentation of these two bacterial types is linked to differences in the virulence and characterics that each bacterium possesses. Characteristics that enhance the virulence of any infectious agent are called virulence factors, and each bacterium contains a unique set of these factors.

the mouth and must travel through the acidity of the stomach to arrive at the intestinal mucosal surface, the primary colonization site. EHEC, for example, has acquired acid resistance, or the ability to survive in extremely acidic environments, by turning on and off specific genes that ease the stress on the cell and enable it to pass through the stomach unscathed.[2] This same ability allows EHEC to survive in acidic foods such as apple juice. In order to move between sites, *E. coli* use flagella, the tail-like structures that propel the bacteria through the body.

Upon exposure to mucosal surfaces, *E. coli* utilizes special structures that initiate colonization. These structures are called **pili** (*pilus,* singular) or **fimbriae** and are arm-like appendages that extend from the bacteria and attach directly to mucous membranes (Figure 6.1). Each *E. coli* type possesses unique fimbrial structures that vary in size and function and are encoded by distinct virulence genes or gene sets.

In order to avoid clearance by immune system cells, the outer membrane of most *E. coli* has a lipopolysaccharide (LPS) region (**O-antigen**). Most of the LPS is conserved, or is encoded by nearly identical genes across different types of *E. coli*, however, each LPS contains a unique region, which predicts the serotype.

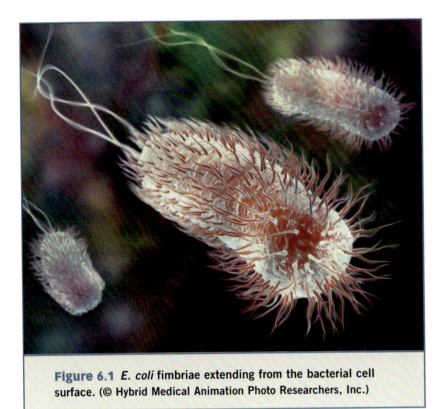

Figure 6.1 *E. coli* fimbriae extending from the bacterial cell surface. (© Hybrid Medical Animation Photo Researchers, Inc.)

Over 170 different serotypes have been described. Prior to the development of more sophisticated genetic methods, the serotype was used to classify *E. coli* strains. Although knowledge of some serotypes (e.g., O157) can provide clues about disease, specific serotypes are not always linked exclusively to certain types of diarrheagenic *E. coli*, for example. Therefore, more definitive characterization is often required.[3] In addition to the LPS, most *E. coli* types also possess capsular polysaccharides (K-antigens) that form an envelope around the cell; the K-antigens vary in type and also are important for evading immune system cells.[4]

Finally, the mechanism by which the different groups of diarrheagenic *E. coli* cause damage to host cells varies considerably (Figure 6.2). Each *E. coli* type carries unique virulence gene combinations that are important for disease development. Most of these virulence genes exist on mobile genetic elements such as **plasmids** and **pathogenicity islands**, that can be transferred between bacteria and get inserted into specific spots in the bacterial chromosome.

EVOLUTION

E. coli have evolved and changed considerably over time. New outbreaks sometimes result because of changes in the virulence or pathogenic potential of old strains, while recombination or genetic exhange, is responsible for the emergence of new genotypes. If these genetic changes enhance a bacterium's survival in some way, then the bacterium will proliferate and increase in frequency relative to other less virulent strains. This process is called **natural selection**. *E. coli* O157:H7, for example, is thought to have evolved from a nonpathogenic strain (O55:H7) by an alteration in its LPS antigen and the acquisition of Shiga toxin genes. Selective pressures present in the environment, foods and people will continue to contribute to the evolution of *E. coli* and it is likely that new pathogenic types will emerge.

ENTEROHEMORRHAGIC *E. COLI* PATHOGENESIS

Both enterohemorrhagic *E. coli* (EHEC) and enteropathogenic *E. coli* (EPEC) have similar methods of adherence to host mucosal surfaces, a critical step in the disease process. Following the initial contact with large intestine cells, EHEC induces a major rearrangement of the host cell to create a pedestal for the bacterium. These pedestals, called attaching and effacing lesions, enable the bacterium to intimately adhere to the cell surface (Figure 6.2).

To develop attaching and effacing lesions, bacterial products encoded by genes located on the locus of enterocyte effacement (LEE) pathogenicity island are required. Collectively, the products trigger the formation of a receptor on the surface of host cells that binds intimin, an important bacterial product encoded by the *eae* gene that facilitates intimate attachment

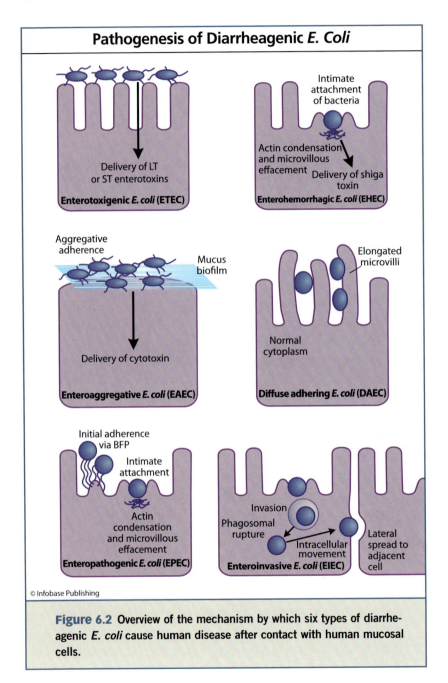

Pathogenesis of Diarrheagenic *E. Coli*

© Infobase Publishing

Figure 6.2 Overview of the mechanism by which six types of diarrheagenic *E. coli* cause human disease after contact with human mucosal cells.

to the cell.[5] This intimate attachment triggers the formation of the attaching and effacing lesions and prevents the bacterium from getting flushed out of the body. Several studies have demonstrated that intimin is critical for lesion formation and the subsequent colonization of the large intestine.[6]

Following colonization, EHEC will produce one or more types of Shiga toxins (Stx), potent toxins that are encoded by genes carried on **bacteriophages**, or viruses that infect bacteria and become incorporated into the bacterial chromosome. There are two main Stx types, Stx1 and Stx2, which can occur alone or together. In addition, numerous Stx variants also have been described; the most notable is Stx2c, a close relative of Stx2 which is encoded by genes present on a distinct bacteriophage.[7] Several studies have demonstrated that certain Stx combinations account for differences in disease severity. For example, a Danish study found that most strains recovered from HUS patients produced Stx2 and/or Stx2c, as did the majority of patients reporting bloody diarrhea.[8] Other studies have reported an association between Stx2c and both HUS and bloody diarrhea, indicating that the Stx combination affects clinical presentation.[9] Similarly, it was demonstrated that EHEC O157 strains belonging to a specific **phylogenetic lineage**, or an evolutionarily related group with similar genetic characteristics, were more common among patients with HUS.[10] Together, these findings demonstrate that infection with a particular type of EHEC strain is an important factor in how disease process progresses, and partly explains why there such a wide range of clinical symptoms reported.

ENTEROPATHOGENIC *E. COLI* PATHOGENESIS

After exposure to small intestine mucosa, typical enteropathogenic *E. coli* (EPEC) will produce an arm-like structure called a bundle-forming pilus that promotes localized adherence, a unique feature of EPEC. The *bfp* gene that encodes the pilus is located on the EPEC adherence factor (EAF) plasmid, that can be transferred between bacteria. Interestingly, atypical EPEC, which has been shown to be increasing in frequency relative to typical EPEC, lacks the EAF plasmid and therefore, does not utilize the bundle-forming pilus for adherence.

For both typical and atypical EPEC strains, the development of attaching and effacing lesions similar to those induced by EHEC is critical for colonization. Both EPEC strain types produce the lesions and also carry the LEE pathogenicity island that encodes intimin and other factors important for intimate attachment. An interesting feature of EPEC is its ability to move from pedestal to pedestal across the exterior of mucosal cells by utilizing compounds present in the human mucosal tissue.[11] Unlike EHEC, however, EPEC strains do not produce Stx or any other potent toxins, a detail that many researchers consider to be puzzling for a pathogen that can cause such severe and persistent disease.

ENTEROTOXIGENIC *E. COLI* PATHOGENESIS

Enterotoxigenic *E. coli* (ETEC) has a very different mechanism of pathogenesis from EHEC and EPEC, that involves the production of colonization factors and two toxins known as the heat-labile enterotoxin and heat-stable enterotoxin. The genes encoding both ETEC toxins (*elt or etx*) are typically located on plasmids that often contain genes for colonization factors as well. More than 20 different **colonization factors** have been described; these factors represent three distinct types of fimbriae and are critical for adherence to the mucosal surface of the small intestine. In addition, the different colonization factors vary in frequency by population and some combinations have been linked to enhanced virulence.[12]

ENTEROAGGREGATIVE *E. COLI* PATHOGENESIS

Little is known about the pathogenesis of enteroaggregative *E. coli* (EAEC) infections, though it was suggested that the characteristic aggregative adherence is thought to occur following attachment and is initiated by two fimbrial structures called the aggregative adherence fimbriae.[13] These fimbriae are responsible for the initial attachment to small intestine mucosal cells and the set of genes that encode them are present on a large plasmid.[14] In addition, EAEC has been shown to stimulate mucus production, which acts as a blanket to trap bacteria, thereby preventing elimination from the body and aiding in persistent colonization.[15] Another key feature of EAEC is the production of a toxin called EAST1 that is encoded by *ast*A which is located on the same plasmid as the fimbriae genes, and has a structure similar to the heat-stable enterotoxin of ETEC.[16] The plasmid carrying these EAEC virulence genes are not found in all EAEC strains, but have been found in some nonpathogenic strains, demonstrating that there is considerable variation in the ability to cause disease between EAEC strains.[17]

ENTEROINVASIVE *E. COLI* PATHOGENESIS

The pathogenesis of enteroinvasive *E. coli* (EIEC) is very different from the other diarrheagenic *E. coli*, but is nearly identical to the pathogenesis of *Shigella*, a close relative. Unlike other diarrheagenic *E. coli*, EIEC has the ability to invade cells, a characteristic that is caused by unique virulence components that are encoded by multiple genes present in the chromosome as well as on a plasmid. The primary virulence genes (*mxi* and *spa*) encode an apparatus that secretes multiple proteins, that contribute to the invasive process.[18] Additionally, EIEC also produces one or more cytotoxins that damage cells, thereby contributing to the development of more severe disease.[19]

To invade colon cells, EIEC attaches to and becomes engulfed by the host cell membrane, which creates a **vacuole**- or a cavity inside a cell enclosed by a membrane. This is a useful mechanism by which bacteria can evade host immune responses because it is surrounded by a host cell membrane. Following release from the vacuole, EIEC will then multiply and infect neighboring cells.[20]

DIFFUSE ADHERING *E. COLI* PATHOGENESIS

The pathogenesis of diffuse adhering *E. coli* (DAEC) infections is not as well studied as the other diarrheagenic *E. coli,* however, the fimbrial structures that mediate the diffuse adherence pattern have been well characterized. Two categories of DAEC have been identified, with one group harboring fimbrial structures containing Dr **adhesins**—the tips of fimbrial structures that attach directly to specific host cells.[21] The Dr adhesins, which are also very common UPEC, are classified based on their ability to bind to human decay accelerating factor (DAF), a protein present on the surface of host cells that prevents the cells from being killed by the immune system. DAEC are also capable of causing UTIs and share similar virulence characteristics with UPEC strains. Instead of Dr adhesins, the other group of DAEC contains a unique fimbrial adhesin called AIDA-I.[22] Moreover, some strains in this group contain genes similar to those found on the LEE pathogenicity island of EHEC and EPEC that promote the synthesis of attaching and effacing lesions.[23]

It was suggested that the characteristic diffuse adherence pattern observed by DAEC is important because it creates finger-like extensions from the cell that can envelop bacteria and allow them to hide from harmful antimicrobial agents and host defenses.[24] Some DAEC strains, particularly those that contain the Dr family of adhesins, are also capable of entering the cell by a complex pathway involving host immune cells; once inside the cell, DAEC survives within a vacuole, though the mechanism by which this contributes to disease is not clear.[25] Infection of neighboring cells, a characteristic common in EIEC, is not thought to occur by DAEC.

UROPATHOGENIC *E. COLI* PATHOGENESIS

UPEC has acquired a unique set of virulence characteristics compared to diarrheagenic *E. coli*. In addition to contributing to the development of UTIs, some key UPEC virulence factors act by enhancing long-term survival and growth in the human body. For example, UPEC expresses siderophores—molecules that are capable of sequestering iron from host cells for survival.[26] Similarly, UPEC has developed distinct mechanisms to evade host immune defenses, thereby enhancing its ability to persistently colonize an individual.[27] A variety of toxins have also been described that are capable of destroying host cells to release nutrients and assist in the spread of bacteria. Such factors, combined with a variety of adherence mechanisms (e.g., adhesins, pilus and fimbrial structures, etc.), work together and allow UPEC to invade the urinary tract and cause cyslitis or pyelonephritis.[28]

7

Diagnosis and Treatment

Although there are many pathogenic *E. coli* types, people typically have some common symptoms such as urinary symptoms, or abdominal cramping and diarrhea. Individuals with more severe illness complain of bloody diarrhea or have symptoms indicative of HUS, sepsis, or meningitis. In some cases, certain individuals present with few or no symptoms, but laboratory testing reveals an infection. Because of the wide range of clinical illness associated with *E. coli* infections, they are often difficult to diagnose without laboratory confirmation. Consequently, health care providers must be able to recognize signs of infection or have knowledge of prior epidemiological exposures to order the appropriate laboratory tests and develop treatment strategies. Rapid diagnosis of pathogenic *E. coli* is imperative to pinpoint the source of the infection, avoid more severe disease from developing, prevent and control outbreaks, and limit secondary transmission.

DETECTION OF DIARRHEAGENIC *E. COLI*

To identify and differentiate the multiple types of diarrheagenic *E. coli* in the laboratory, a wide variety of methods are employed. Some examples include culturing on specific growth media, assessing biochemical profiles, serotyping, and screening for the presence of virulence characteristics. These methods are either phenotypic, distinguishing strains based on appearance and expression of distinct bacterial features, or genotypic, distinguishing strains based on unique genetic characteristics. The use of these methods, however, varies depending on the laboratory because not all labs have the same capabilities. In fact, many health care facilities in the United States do not even have laboratories and are therefore required to send *E. coli* strains or stool specimens directly to a **reference laboratory** for further evaluation.

Because the prevalence of diarrheagenic *E. coli* types varies by geographic location, screening practices also will vary depending on the common types observed in a given setting. Some laboratories in developing countries may routinely screen for *E. coli* types endemic to the region (e.g., ETEC, EPEC, EAEC ad EIEC), but will not attempt to identify those types that are less prevalent (e.g., EHEC O157:H7).

Bacterial Culture

The culturing techniques that Escherich initially used to identify *E. coli* in the 1800s are still used today. Although new molecular techniques have been developed to more rapidly and reliably identify pathogenic *E. coli*, these methods do not result in a pure bacterial culture. Having a pure culture enables further analysis of the bacterium that is causing a specific infection. For example, assessing antibiotic resistance is difficult without a culture as is DNA isolation for genotyping to determine if bacteria isolated from multiple people are related (i.e., during outbreaks). Consequently, culturing is a highly recommended practice.

To culture bacteria from a clinical **specimen** (e.g., stool, urine, blood), a small amount is transferred to a specific type of growth medium that has been shown to enhance the growth of a given bacterium to facilitate detection. Because *E. coli* are capable of fermentation—the conversion of energy-rich carbohydrates and sugars in the absence of oxygen, certain media types are used that take advantage of this characteristic. **MacConkey agar** or eosin methylene-blue agar is used for most diarrheagenic *E. coli* except *E. coli* O157:H7, and are typically recovered following overnight incubation at 37°C without oxygen. **Bacterial colonies**, or groups of bacteria that grow from a single parent cell, can be seen on the culture plate, and those with the appearance of *E. coli* are selected for additional testing to confirm or rule out *E. coli* infection.

If *E. coli* O157:H7 infection is suspected, culture on **sorbitol** MacConkey (SMAC) agar is common (Figure 7.1).

EHEC O157:H7 strains lack the ability to ferment sorbitol and appear colorless on SMAC, whereas non-pathogenic *E. coli* strains appear red because of sorbitol-fermenting capabilities. Additional phenotypic and genotypic tests are warranted if colorless bacterial colonies are detected on SMAC, particularly

THE ROLE OF A REFERENCE LABORATORY

A reference laboratory, which is often government operated, provides support for hospitals and health care clinics that do not have the ability or finances to evaluate their own laboratory specimens. Most states have one main laboratory, or state health agency, and numerous other smaller reference laboratories located in distinct geographic areas. The state laboratories are critical components of the public health system.

One example is the Michigan Department of Community Health Bureau of Laboratories (MDCH-BOL), housed in Lansing, Michigan. It is the fifth oldest state laboratory in the nation. It was established in 1907, when the Michigan State Board of Health appointed a bacteriologist to examine blood, sputum, urine, water, milk, and any other substance associated with disease outbreaks.

Today, the MDCH-BOL provides laboratory support for many departments within the MDCH; 49 local health departments from different regions in Michigan; other state health departments in the Midwest; and hospitals and health care providers throughout the state. Additionally, MDCH-BOL works closely with the CDC on outbreak investigations, research, and disease prevention programs.

The MDCH-BOL is comprised of numerous sections and the microbiology section is responsible for processing those specimens associated with bacterial infections, including EHEC.

if the patient is symptomatic and/or is epidemiologically linked to a contaminated source or patient previously diagnosed with the infection.

Non-O157 EHEC is similar to non-pathogenic *E. coli* in that it ferments sorbitol; therefore, it is often not detected when using SMAC unless a health care provider requests additional phenotypic or genotypic testing based on patient symptoms or epidemiological data. Consequently, the prevalence of non-O157 EHEC is often underestimated because of the difficulties associated with culturing. The same is true for a subpopulation of EHEC O157 that is capable of fermenting sorbitol; these strains are not common in the United States, but cause a large proportion of diarrheal disease and HUS in other countries, particularly Germany.

Biochemical Characteriztion

Even though trained microbiologists can easily identify *E. coli* on MAC and other media, more specific biochemical tests must be conducted for confirmation. A spot **indole** test for example, is often used to rule out the presence of other enteric bacteria such as *Salmonella* and *Shigella*. Virtually all *E. coli* produce indole, which causes a spot indole test solution to turn purple.

Serotyping

Determining the type of O-antigen (somatic) and **H-antigen** (flagellar) that a specific bacterial strain possesses is an important phenotypic trait of *E. coli* that has been examined in the laboratory since the 1940s. EHEC strains of the O157:H7 serotype, for example, have the 157th type of O-antigen and the seventh type of flagellar antigen. Agglutination tests, or methods that detect the interaction of specific O-type **antibodies** with the corresponding **antigen** present in a bacterium, are commonly used to characterize the O-antigen of *E. coli* strains. The H types can be differentiated in the same way or by genotypic methods that examine genetic variation in the gene that

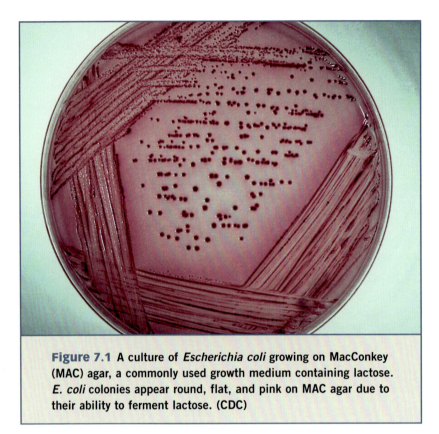

Figure 7.1 A culture of *Escherichia coli* growing on MacConkey (MAC) agar, a commonly used growth medium containing lactose. *E. coli* colonies appear round, flat, and pink on MAC agar due to their ability to ferment lactose. (CDC)

encodes the H-antigen. Currently, over 170 distinct O-antigens have been identified as have over 55 H-antigen types.

Knowledge of the serotype provides clues about the *E. coli* type causing an infection, particularly for those genotypes not easily identified via culture and those that are common causes of outbreaks. In addition to inaccurately categorizing diarrheagenic *E. coli* strains, serotyping is also labor intensive, costly, and performed by only a few reference laboratories nationwide.[1] The development of rapid serotyping kits has therefore been useful for cutting costs and labor, particularly for EHEC O157; however, most laboratories will also examine suspect bacteria for other phenotypic and/or genotypic features characteristic of the different *E. coli* types.

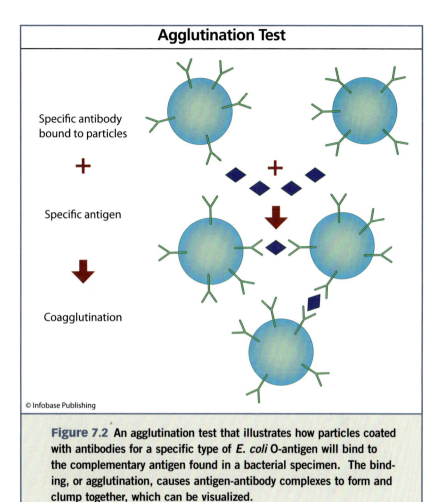

Agglutination Test

Specific antibody
bound to particles

+

Specific antigen

Coagglutination

© Infobase Publishing

Figure 7.2 An agglutination test that illustrates how particles coated with antibodies for a specific type of *E. coli* O-antigen will bind to the complementary antigen found in a bacterial specimen. The binding, or agglutination, causes antigen-antibody complexes to form and clump together, which can be visualized.

Evalution of Cellular Adherence Patterns

Because some types of diarrheagenic *E. coli* cause distinct patterns of adherence to epithelial cells during infection, human epithelial cell (HEp)-2 adherence assays are often used for detection and differentiation. These adherence assays involve infecting HEp-2 cells with a bacterial culture, incubating at 37°C with 5% CO_2, and washing and staining the cells for visualization via a microscope. If EPEC is present, then a localized adherence pattern is observed, while an aggregative adherence pattern is observed for EAEC infections and a diffuse adherence pattern for DAEC infections.[2]

Production of Virulence Components

An enzyme immunoassay (EIA) is a phenotypic test that facilitates the detection of a bacterial product. The concept is similar to that of an agglutination test except that the antigen-antibody complex is recognized by another antibody linked to an enzyme that catalyzes the reaction mixture and causes a color change (Figure 7.3). Such a change is indicative of the presence of the bacterial product.

To confirm an EHEC infection, for example, an EIA is commonly used that targets the Shiga toxin (Stx). The Stx EIA is capable of detecting the presence of Stx in stool specimens and can be used in conjunction with culturing. To perform an EIA, microbiologists use a microtiter plate containing 96 wells that are coated with Stx antibodies. If Stx is present in a stool specimen, then it will bind to the Stx antibodies coating the well and the solution will change colors. Because the EIA detects the presence of Stx directly, strains of all serotypes, including non-O157 EHEC, can be identified. This represents an advantage over bacterial culturing on SMAC agar, which is not useful for the detection of non-O157 serotypes. Despite this, the EIA is relatively costly and not all laboratories can afford to use it on a regular basis.

Virulence Gene Screening

Numerous genotypic tests have been developed that target unique virulence characteristics of different diarrheagenic *E. coli* in an effort to more reliably and efficiently identify and differentiate the genotypes in the laboratory. The use of these tests, however, varies by geographic location, as some regions have differing frequencies of each *E. coli* type than others. In the United States, most clinical laboratories will rule out an EHEC infection before screening for other diarrheagenic *E. coli* types, while some developing countries may choose to initially screen for ETEC. The use of the **polymerase chain reaction (PCR)**, for instance, enables the identification of specific virulence genes by screening for segments of DNA sequence unique to an *E. coli* type. The EHEC Shiga toxin genes that encode Stx1, Stx2, and additional Stx variants, represent good candidates for differentiating EHEC from the other diarrheagenic *E. coli* types. In fact, many clinical laboratories commonly use PCR methods to identify Stx genes in bacterial strains isolated from stool samples. This method is particularly useful for detecting non-O157 EHEC, as it is often overlooked on culture plates.

Many additional virulence gene targets have been used in PCR methods including *eaeA, bfpA,* and EAF (EPEC); *invE* (EIEC); *elt, estp,* and *esth* (ETEC); and CVD432 and *aggR* (EAggEC). Both single and multiplex PCR methods, which allow the simultaneous detection of up to 12 genes, have been developed.[3]

Detection of Non-diarrheagenic *E. Coli*

To detect UPEC from patients with UTIs, bacterial culturing is used in conjunction with other laboratory tests. Patients suspected of having a UTI will submit urine specimens for evalution. A small quantity of urine is transferred to a growth medium, incubated overnight at 37°C, and evaluated for the total number of bacterial colonies—or colony forming units (CFU) per milliliter (ml) of urine. A patient is considered to have a UTI caused by UPEC if: (1) the culture is predominantly comprised of UPEC with few other bacterial types present; (2) the number of UPEC exceeds 10^2 CFU/ml; and (3) the patient is complaining of urinary symptoms (e.g., increased frequency of urination, urgency to urinate, back or flank pain, burning, etc.). A patient is considered to have asymptomatic bacteriuria if the number of UPEC exceeds 10^5 CFU/ml and the patient reports no symptoms.

In addition to the bacterial culture results, health care providers typically evaluate urine for the presence and quantity of white blood cells (leukocytes), which are responsible for fighting infections. Detecting an elevated number of leukocytes can be easily done with urinalysis. The urinalysis involves testing a clean catch, midstream urine specimen for an elevated number of red blood cells and nitrates in addition to leukocytes, all of which are indicative of a UTI. In cases where patients are reporting more severe symptoms, blood cultures are performed to determine whether bacteria have entered the bloodstream,

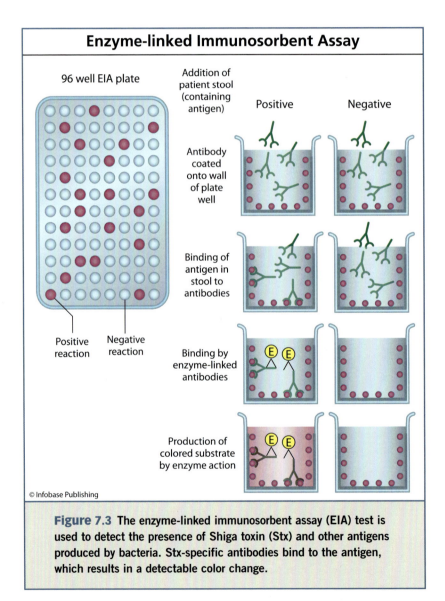

Figure 7.3 The enzyme-linked immunosorbent assay (EIA) test is used to detect the presence of Shiga toxin (Stx) and other antigens produced by bacteria. Stx-specific antibodies bind to the antigen, which results in a detectable color change.

and an examination of products (e.g., creatinine) indicative of kidney function is occasionally warranted. Blood and cerebrospinal fluid cultures also are utilized in newborn babies suspected of having *E. coli* sepsis or meningitis.

TREATING *E. COLI* INFECTIONS

Similar to other bacterial infections, **antibiotics**—or substances that have the capability of killing or preventing the growth of bacteria—can be used to treat *E. coli* infections. This is common practice for UPEC UTIs, bloodstream infections, and meningitis in neonates; however, there is considerable debate regarding the use of antibiotics for treating infections caused by diarrheagenic *E. coli*. Most symptoms caused by EHEC, for example, are caused by the production of Shiga toxin (Stx); therefore, it is possible that giving a patient a substance that causes bacterial cell death contributes to an increased release of Stx and more severe disease. Some studies have demonstrated that antibiotic use actually facilitates HUS development, though this has not been shown in all studies.[4] The treatment of HUS is extensive and can involve renal transplantation in severe cases. By contrast, antibiotic use has been shown to be useful for treating diarrheal disease caused by both ETEC and EPEC. Nevertheless, detailed studies of antibiotic use for EIAC, EAEC and DAEC infections have not been conducted. Although travelers to endemic regions are often given antibiotics to take to prevent an infection, people living in developing countries where ETEC and EPEC infections are common cannot take antibiotics all the time, as antibiotics are in limited supply, are costly, and contribute to major disturbances in the normal flora by killing beneficial microbes. Furthermore, the practice can lead to the development of antibiotic resistance.

ANTIBIOTIC RESISTANCE

Because so many bacterial infections are treated with antibiotics, many bacteria have evolved ways to resist the killing mechanism of antibiotics. This is referred to as **antibiotic resistance**. Some bacteria are naturally resistant and possess efflux pumps that can pump certain antibiotics out of the cell to avoid cell death, while other bacteria have acquired mutations or genes that enable the bacterium to resist antibiotic activity. Such mutations can occur independently within a bacterium, but in most cases, resistance genes present on mobile DNA segments (e.g., plasmids) get transferred from one bacterium to another.

For *E. coli*, antibiotic resistance has become more common, which is due in part to the overuse and misuse of antibiotics. Patients who do not take the entire course of antibiotics as prescribed by a health care provider, for example, can contribute to resistance development by exposing bacteria to a low level of drug, thereby making it easier for bacteria to survive in the presence of the drug. Because bacteria divide and proliferate so rapidly, low levels of antibiotics can "turn on" specific genes located on an acquired plasmid, for instance, that promote resistance. As the concentration of antibiotic required to kill bacteria becomes higher, full resistance can develop and the drug will no longer be effective. Using antibiotics can also select from strains of bacteria that have resistance mechanisms. Antibiotics also are commonly used on farms and hence, resistance has developed among common colonizing bacteria (e.g., EHEC O157:H7) residing in farm animals. If entry into the food chain occurs, then these resistant bacteria can be passed on to people.

The prevalence of antibiotic resistance among diarrheagenic *E. coli* ranges from 37 to 63% for many of the antibiotics that are commonly used to treat *E. coli* infections.[5] Furthermore, it was estimated that more than 89% of diarrheagenic *E. coli* are resistant to more than one antibiotic, referred to as **multidrug resistance**.[6] Similar frequencies also have been identified for UPEC strains that cause UTIs, particularly in women with frequently recurring infections.[7] Cases of multidrug resistant *E. coli* causing bloodstream infections are also increasing in frequency and were found to be associated with higher death rates and longer hospital stays.[8]

Antibiotic resistance is a global concern that contributes to higher health care costs and death rates, treatment failures, and a longer duration of clinical illness. The identification and development of novel antimicrobial agents is therefore critical for managing bacterial infections in the future. For developing countries, the negative impact associated with antibiotic resistance is much greater since alternative antibiotics are not readily available and these countries typically lack the public health infrastructure required to combat resistant infections.

ALTERNATIVE THERAPIES

In addition to antibiotics, alternative treatment methods are also used for diarrheal diseases caused by *E. coli*. Many deaths attributable to diarrheal diseases result from the severe dehydration that accompanies an infection. This is particularly true for young children, who get dehydrated more easily. Oral rehydration therapy is often used to replace the nutrients and electrolytes lost through diarrhea, but intravenous rehydration is necessary in more severe cases. Some over-the-counter medications, including bismuth subsalicylate (Pepto-Bismol) and loperamide (Immodium), have been shown to decrease the severity of diarrhea, but are only recommended for mild cases. The administration of bovine milk antibodies targeting EPEC has also been effective.[9]

Because diarrheal diseases cause so many deaths among babies and children worldwide, the development of treatment guidelines that decrease the disease burden are critical. Some topics that were incorporated into treatment guidelines developed by the World Health Organization (WHO) include promoting rapid and effective treatments, increasing the recognition of symptoms associated with severe disease, improving management of infections at home, and providing education on malnutrition risks and prevention practices (e.g. breastfeeding). By incorporating these guidelines into the management and treatment of diarrheal diseases, the lives of many could be saved each year.

8

Disease Prevention

Identifying the source or cause of an *E. coli* infection is extremely important for preventing new disease cases from occurring and decreasing the likelihood of an outbreak. Case investigations, particularly during an outbreak, present research and training opportunities and often provide justification for making public, political and/or legal changes to prevent future infections. Such investigations also grant the opportunity to evaluate the effectiveness of current surveillance systems and establish new guidelines and control methods. The major *E. coli* O157:H7 outbreaks of the 1980s and early 1990s, for example, underscored the need for outbreak prevention efforts. Because *E. coli* O157:H7 resides in farm animals, food products, water, and the farm environment, a complicated prevention strategy is required. Most public health officials believe that the farm represents the best site for prevention efforts because animals that are not colonized with *E. coli* O157:H7 do not run the risk of contaminating meat or the water supply. Others, however, disagree with this argument, claiming that the food industry should be responsible for preventing bacterial contamination of food items.

Instead of placing the responsibility on one institution or industry, the U.S. Department of Agriculture (USDA) has adopted a farm-to-table strategy for preventing foodborne illnesses. This approach recognizes that prevention efforts will work best if individuals from different sectors of industry and society, including consumers, work together to decrease the likelihood of food contamination. Enterohemorrhagic *E. coli* (EHEC) represents a group of bacteria that commonly contaminate the farm environment and food supply and therefore, many disease prevention practices have been developed to prevent contamination.

ENTEROHEMORRHAGIC *E. COLI* IN THE FOOD SUPPLY

In October 1994, the USDA created an organization called the Food Safety and Inspection Service (FSIS), which is responsible for regulating and inspecting meat, poultry, and egg products to ensure that they are safe and correctly labeled. In 2001, FSIS inspected more than 8.2 billion poultry, 140 million heads of livestock, and 4.5 billion pounds of eggs. FSIS also monitors foreign inspection systems before allowing other countries to export meat or poultry products to the United States. Those products allowed to enter are always reinspected upon arrival.

For livestock, inspectors examine animals before and after slaughter to prevent any contaminated meat from being processed. Inspections are conducted randomly at more than 1,700 meat-processing plants and 100,000 retail stores distributed throughout the nation. About 250,000 other meat products, including frozen dinners, soups, sausages, and pizzas, are also inspected regularly.[1]

Prior to the creation of FSIS, federal regulations involving meat inspection were less than perfect. In fact, some refer to the old technique of bacterial detection as the "sniff-based" method, in which only foul-smelling meat products were eliminated from processing. Today, science-based procedures are used, which rely on more sensitive microbiological testing methods to identify and culture bacterial contaminants. In 2008, for example, FSIS analyzed 11,230 samples of raw ground beef for *E. coli* O157:H7 contamination; 53 samples were positive. If bacterial contamination is present, FSIS will typically institute a recall, or the voluntary removal of contaminated products from the market in an effort to prevent foodborne infections.

For meat, the recall process is made easier because products have a date code, lot number, and, often, a store number, which enables inspectors to locate the contaminated products rapidly. In most situations, however, this is a difficult process, because multiple processing plants, retail stores, and restaurants are often involved. In April 2003, for instance, Umpqua Indian Foods of Oregon voluntarily recalled 180 lbs. (82 kg) of ground beef with suspected *E. coli* O157:H7 contamination detected by FSIS inspectors. Although each package of ground beef contained specific dates and lot numbers, there was no way to track all of the meat. In situations like this, FSIS relies heavily on the media and state and local health departments to inform citizens, stores, and restaurant owners of the recall and the potential health risks.

The USDA recall classification system is composed of three classes — Class I, II, and III — that differ based on the health risks to humans.[2]

> **Class I:** A health hazard situation where there is reasonable probability that the use of the recalled product will cause serious adverse health consequences or death.
>
> **Class II:** A health hazard situation where there is a remote probability of adverse health consequences from use of the recalled product.
>
> **Class III:** A situation where the use of the product will not cause adverse health consequences.

For *E. coli* O157:H7 contamination, a Class I or II recall is generally instituted. One of the largest recalls associated with *E. coli* O157:H7 contamination in the history of the United States occurred in 1997, when Hudson Foods Company of Arkansas recalled 25 million lbs. (11.3 million kg) of frozen ground beef patties. The FSIS learned of the contaminated ground beef after 14 consumers got sick and reported eating the meat to the Colorado Department of Public Health and Environment. The quick, voluntary action of Hudson Foods to institute a recall was critical in preventing further infections.[3] Despite the control efforts utilized by the FSIS that target the beef processing industry, *E. coli* O157:H7 contamination still occurs. In 2007, the FSIS recommended recalls for 21 different beef products, 10 of which were associated with human infection. Because these numbers represented an increase relative to previous years, it is clear that additional control efforts are required.[4]

Table 8.1 Points of intervention to decrease *E. coli* O157:H7 contamination of the food supply

Point of intervention for *E. coli* O157:H7	Example of intervention strategy
Decrease colonization and fecal shedding frequency among cattle	1. Adding beneficial bacteria to farm feed to compete with *E. coli* O157:H7 or kill it. 2. Innovative vaccines containing *E. coli* O157:H7 virulence genes that stimulate an immune response in the gastro-intestinal tract of cattle. 3. Bacterial viruses that kill certain bacteria (e.g., bacteriophages). 4. Farm management practices (e.g., avoid using feedlots, diet changes).
Decrease contamination in drinking water	1. Frequent cleaning (e.g., remove biofilms that trap the bacterium). 2. Remove sediments from water troughs.
Decrease contamination in manure	1. Add beneficial bacteria to kill *E. coli* O157:H7 present in farmyard. 2. Add beneficial bacteria to kill *E. coli* O157:H7 present in manure compost. 3. Adopt management practices that allow cow manure to be used only as a fertilizer for soil and not other types of produce.
Improve personal hygiene of animal handlers	1. Educate handlers about handwashing, fecal-oral transmission, and CDC guidelines. 2. Ensure that farm visitors do not contact animals and manure. Educate others about handwashing if contact occurs

Source: Michael P. Doyle of the University of Georgia Center for Food Safety. Available online at http://www.fsis.usda.gov.

ENTEROHEMORRHAGIC *E. COLI* IN THE AGRICULTURE INDUSTRY

Farm prevention strategies are quite complex because so many different factors contribute to EHEC colonization and contamination of cattle. Thus, numerous points of intervention have been identified that can potentially have an impact on the level of bacterial contamination at a given farm (Table 8.1). Though many researchers have implemented and evaluated prevention programs targeting farms, few have been successful at significantly decreasing the amount of *E. coli* O157:H7 contamination. A few studies that yielded positive results are highlighted here.

Decreasing Colonization in Cattle

By decreasing the frequency of EHEC colonization within a herd, it is also possible to decrease the level of contamination in food and the farm environment, thereby reducing the frequency of human disease. One study demonstrated that feeding cattle beneficial bacteria such as *Lactobacilli,* which are common in yogurt and are capable of outcompeting other bacteria in the gut (Figure 8.1), reduced the degree of fecal shedding of EHEC in cattle by 74%. A 74% decrease in the level of hide contamination also was observed.[5] This use of **probiotics**, or bacteria that can be ingested and have a beneficial effect on the host by preventing infection with other pathogenic microorganisms, has increased significantly over the years and represents a promising mechanism for decreasing contamination in cattle.

Another intervention that can potentially decrease fecal shedding in cattle involves vaccination. Several EHEC vaccines targeting proteins encoded by the locus of enterocyte effacement (LEE) genes as well as other virulence components important for colonization have been tested in cattle. Two recent studies, for example, demonstrated that vaccinated cattle challenged with *E. coli* O157 had lower levels of colonization than nonvaccinated cattle, with one of the studies reporting a 92% decrease in colonization among the vaccinated group.[6] Consequently, vaccination in cattle also represents a promising strategy for reducing the level of contamination on farms.

An alternative to probiotics and vaccination is the use of bacteriophages, which are viruses that have the ability to target and destroy specific bacterial types. One study demonstrated the successful use of phage therapy in preventing and treating ETEC infections in newborn farm animals. Phages that target other foodborne bacteria, including *E. coli* O157:H7, have yet to be described, but may also be helpful. More research is

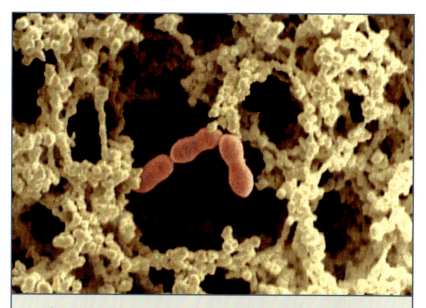

Figure 8.1 The photomicrograph shows the structure of yogurt. Different types of Lactobacillus bacteria (pink) are added to milk to make yogurt. When people eat them, these bacteria are beneficial because they reside in the gut and can prevent other harmful agents from invading and causing disease. Often, health care providers advise patients to eat yogurt if they are suffering from a gastrointestinal infection or have taken antibiotics that are known to kill the normal bacteria that live in the gut. (© Visuals Unlimited)

required, however, to determine how to select specific phages for use, examine ways to administer therapy, and evaluate the impact of phage evolution and resistance indifferent bacteria.[7]

Finally, many farms have turned to antibiotic use in an effort to decrease fecal shedding and colonization frequencies. Most studies that have examined the effect of antibiotic use on shedding have concluded that antibiotics make no difference. Indeed, several studies have actually identified an increased frequency of fecal shedding following the addition of antibiotics to cattle feed, while others have demonstrated colonization with antibiotic resistant *E. coli*.[8] One study, for example, found that 7.5% of sampled cattle carried *E. coli* strains that were resistant to common antibiotics, and that resistance occurred more frequently in *E. coli* O157:H7 than *E. coli* of the normal flora.[9]

Preventing Water Contamination

A very simple intervention process, such as cleaning water troughs and removing contaminated sediments, may significantly decrease the frequency of EHEC O157:H7 on farms.

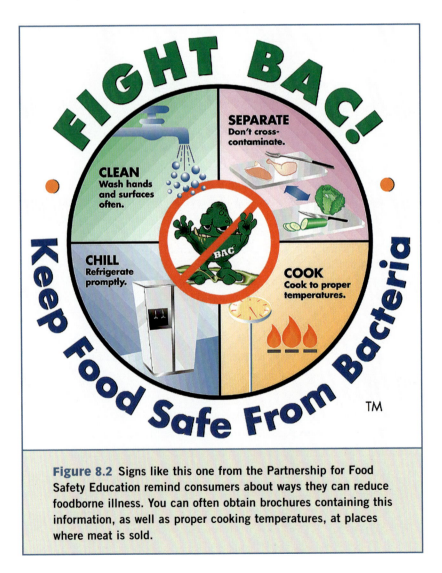

Figure 8.2 Signs like this one from the Partnership for Food Safety Education remind consumers about ways they can reduce foodborne illness. You can often obtain brochures containing this information, as well as proper cooking temperatures, at places where meat is sold.

PREPARING MEAT FOR CONSUMPTION

Meat should always be prepared following very specific instructions. It may appear to be suitable for consumption, but meat can easily be contminated with bacterial pathogens. During meat preparation, bacteria can be transferred to other food items while preparing other foods in a process called cross-contamination.

(continues)

FOOD	°F
Ground Meat & Meat Mixtures	
Beef, Pork, Veal, Lamb	160
Turkey, Chicken	165
Fresh Beef, Veal, Lamb	
Medium Rare	145
Medium	160
Well Done	170
Poultry	
Chicken & Turkey, whole	180
Poultry breasts, roast	170
Poultry thighs, wings	180
Duck & Goose	180
Stuffing (cooked alone or in a bird)	165
Fresh Pork	
Medium	160
Well Done	170
Ham	
Fresh (raw)	160
Pre-cooked (to reheat)	140
Eggs & Egg Dishes	
Eggs	Cook until yolk & white are firm
Egg dishes	160
Leftovers & Casseroles	165

The following simple steps are recommended while preparing meat.

First, hands should be washed with soap and water before and after preparing meat. After cutting up and preparing meat, cross-contamination can be prevented by washing cutting boards, counter surfaces, dishes, and utensils in soapy water before reusing them. Raw meat juices should never mix with other food items. Marinades used on raw meat, for example, should be discarded and not used again on cooked meat. In addition, meat should be cooked thoroughly; a red or pink color indicates that the meat is raw or undercooked and that cooking temperatures may not have been high enough to kill any bacteria that might be present. Hamburgers, in particular, should be cooked to an internal temperature of at least 165°F (74°C). A meat thermometer is the best way to be sure food has reached the proper internal temperature.

One investigation that took place on four Wisconsin dairy farms, for example, involved sampling 15 calves for an entire year. Interestingly, when the drinking water troughs became contaminated with *E. coli* O157:H7, exposed cattle quickly became colonized and began to shed the bacterium in their feces, causing it to spread rapidly throughout the herd.[9]

By contrast, interventions that involve decontaminating water are not as simple. For EHEC and ETEC, runoff containing contaminated fecal matter from cattle farms can get into the groundwater and nearby streams, rivers and lakes. Because *E. coli* O157:H7 can survive for weeks in water, has a low infectious dose (the amount needed to cause disease in an individual), and several large-scale outbreaks have occurred

THE IMPORTANCE OF REFRIGERATION

A large portion of the eastern United States experienced a major power outage in August 2003 that left millions of residents without electricity for one to two days. During that time, numerous advisories were issued to residents living in certain areas to boil water before drinking and to throw out spoiled food. The reason behind these advisories was to prevent food-borne and waterborne infections. In Detroit, for example, the water advisories were issued because the power outage had shut down water-processing plants, and therefore, sewage-contaminated water could potentially enter drinking water. In this situation, residents were told to boil water for 10 minutes and allow it to cool completely before drinking it.[a]

The food advisory was issued because bacteria can multiply rapidly in meat and poultry when the temperature rises above 40°F (4.4°C). For refrigerated and frozen foods, particularly meat, the refrigeration temperature should always be kept at or below 40°F (4.4°C), while a freezer should not fall below 0°F (-17.8°C). In the event of a power outage or other emergency, the refrigerator and freezer doors should be kept closed to maintain the appropriate temperature. Food should be thrown away if the power is out for more than four hours for a refrigerator or 48 hours for a freezer.

The FSIS recommends that residents always be prepared for emergency situations by having food items on hand that do not require refrigeration. When the electricity returns, frozen food can be refrozen only if the food still contains ice crystals or if the food temperature is lower than 40°F (4.4°C). When in doubt about the safety of a food item, however, it is always wise to throw it away. Warmer temperatures enable potentially harmful bacteria, such as E. coli O157:H7, to thrive.

a. Foodsafety.gov. "Gateway to Government Food Safety Information: Consumer Advice on Disaster Assistance." 2003. Available online at http://www.foodsafety.gov.

as a result of exposure to contaminated water, the testing of waters used for recreational purposes has become standard practice in the United States. The same is true for drinking water. In developing countries, however, water contamination is an even bigger problem since many countries lack the finances, infrastructure and sanitation required to deliver clean water to residents.

RETAILERS AND CONSUMERS

Meat sold to retail stores is not inspected by FSIS, but rather is examined randomly by local and state inspectors. Because of this, FSIS works with a separate organization called the Association of Food and Drug Officials (AFDO), whose job is to focus on educating retailers about foodborne disease risks. AFDO provides an educational course on meat and poultry processing at various sites around the country. The course trains individuals who regulate and inspect retail stores on the hazards associated with grinding and slicing meat, making sausage and dried meat (e.g., jerky), and the curing and smoking processes.

Consumers are the best targets for prevention practices, since they are most at risk for developing a foodborne infection. Many organizations and educational programs focus on consumers. For example, an International Food Safety Council named September National Food Safety Education month, in an effort to heighten awareness about the importance of food safety. The USDA also designed the Food Safety Mobile, a colorful education and outreach vehicle that travels around the United States to teach consumers about the risks associated with mishandling food and to explain useful prevention practices for reducing the risk of foodborne illness.

Future Possibilities and Concerns

THE POSSIBILITIES

The past few decades have seen a major increase in research devoted to *E. coli* infections, particularly the types that contribute to diarrheal disease. Because *E. coli* O157:H7 was only discovered in 1982, there is still much to learn about the bacterium and the severe disease it causes. Many researchers as well as government agencies are devoting a significant amount of time and money to the implementation of prevention programs and innovative technologies that target EHEC in particular. These efforts are extremely important for disease eradication. This chapter will highlight some of the more important developments.

Vaccines

As discussed previously, the administration of vaccines to cattle represents a promising way to decrease fecal shedding and colonization with pathogenic *E. coli*. Because of the difficulties associated with the administration of traditional vaccines to cattle, scientists have begun to explore edible vaccines. A study conducted on volunteers who ate potato vaccines, for example, found that the vaccine elicited an immune response and resulted in the development of *E. coli* antibodies (Figure 9.1). The potato vaccine is a genetically modified potato containing genes that encode for factors (e.g., heat-labile toxin) that are associated with an ETEC infection.

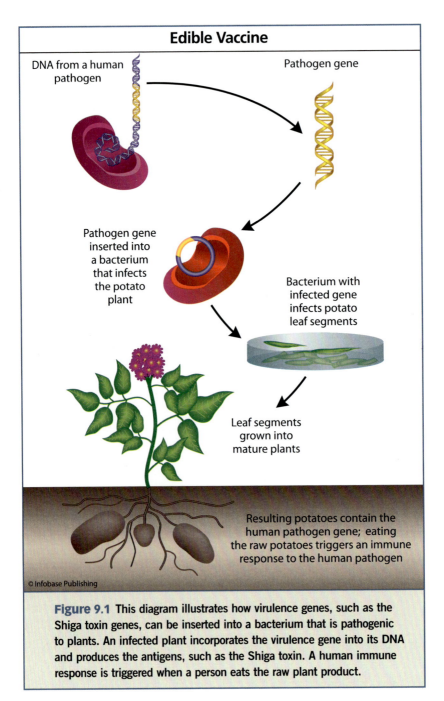

Edible Vaccine

DNA from a human pathogen

Pathogen gene

Pathogen gene inserted into a bacterium that infects the potato plant

Bacterium with infected gene infects potato leaf segments

Leaf segments grown into mature plants

Resulting potatoes contain the human pathogen gene; eating the raw potatoes triggers an immune response to the human pathogen

© Infobase Publishing

Figure 9.1 This diagram illustrates how virulence genes, such as the Shiga toxin genes, can be inserted into a bacterium that is pathogenic to plants. An infected plant incorporates the virulence gene into its DNA and produces the antigens, such as the Shiga toxin. A human immune response is triggered when a person eats the raw plant product.

Better Detection Methods

In addition to cattle, *E. coli* vaccines are also under development for use in human populations. Because of the high degree of genetic diversity and ongoing evolution of most *E. coli* types, effective vaccines must provide broad levels of protection that target multiple virulence components. Promising vaccine candidates have been identified for ETEC that protect adult travelers against diarrhea, however, none of these have been useful in young children, the most important group with the highest frequency of severe disease.[1] Future work must focus on vaccine candidates that are effective in multiple populations. To properly treat various *E. coli* types that cause diarrheal disease, clinical laboratories must first be able to identify the type of *E. coli* in a given specimen. Using current techniques, this is often difficult. Some researchers are now focusing on new ways to detect and isolate bacteria, such as EHEC, using sophisticated molecular methods as well as simple biochemical analyses. A biochemical analysis, for instance, requires that researchers evaluate the specific biochemical profiles of all EHEC strains. This methodology will enable researchers to determine if one biochemical component could be targeted and used for detection. New growth media that distinguish among *E. coli* types also needs to be evaluated. Such enhanced detection systems are important to more accurately and rapidly identify the types of bacterial pathogen, which has serious implications for patient treatment.

Antimicrobials

In August 2003, the Food and Drug Administration (FDA) announced that a Salt Lake City, Utah, company called aLF Ventures would be marketing a new product—a spray containing **lactoferrin**, a naturally occurring antimicrobial agent found in milk. The company demonstrated that spraying lactoferrin on raw beef carcasses inhibited the growth of *E. coli* and prevented the bacterium from attaching to meat surfaces.

A new therapy called Synsorb-Pk is also being considered to combat EHEC infections. Synsorb-Pk is a chemically synthesized compound that has the ability to absorb Shiga toxins in the intestine. It could potentially be used in young children with bloody diarrhea in an effort to decrease the likelihood of HUS development.[2]

THE CONCERNS

Although new detection and prevention methods are continuously being sought, bacteria are constantly changing and evolving over time. Natural selection contributes to the enhancement of certain *E. coli* strains, selecting those mutations that give the bacterium an advantage in the environment. There is always a possibility that some pathogenic *E. coli* strains will become more pathogenic by acquiring different virulence factors or antibiotic resistance genes, for instance. This is also true for nonpathogenic *E. coli* strains present in the normal flora. Such genetic changes can result in large scale epidemics, particularly if immunity levels are low in a given population.

Bioterrorism

Recently, the U.S. federal government has invested billions of dollars to protect our nation from acts of **bioterrorism**—the use of bacteria, viruses, or the toxins produced by them as weapons. Although an act of bioterrorism is not predictable, a high level of public health preparedness can significantly affect the outcome. In January 2002, for example, the USDA received $328 million in government funding for biosecurity measures, or plans to protect the nation from the deliberate release of pathogenic biological agents, such as anthrax. Approximately $10 million of this money was allocated for the development of a food safety bioterrorism protection program. Because EHEC O157:H7 has a low infectious dose and causes such severe disease, it has been suggested to represent an important agent of bioterrorism.

CONCLUSION

Foodborne and waterborne infections are major concerns because they pose a threat to human health and the economy of affected states and nations. In the United States alone, the cost associated with all foodborne disease is estimated to be at least $35 billion a year. Though the incidence of worldwide foodborne disease is difficult to measure, the World Health Organization estimated that diarrheal diseases contributed to 2 to 3 million deaths worldwide in 2004,[3] with many attributable to diarrheagenic *E. coli*.

Complex prevention efforts, which rely on interactions between governments, the food industry, and consumers, are needed to control the pathogens that thrive in food and water. Unfortunately, this is not an easy task, especially with regard to *E. coli*, a ubiquitous bacterium that comes in both pathogenic and nonpathogenic varieties.

For *E. coli* O157:H7, estimates from 2003 suggested that the incidence of infection in the Untied States was decreasing, however, this decrease has not been maintained. Although many control measures have helped, the evolution of EHEC enables its survival in new food vehicles and therefore, control measures must continuously be updated. Another challenge is to maintain the current level of control in the United States, while focusing on other nations that are disproportionately affected by *E. coli*–associated diarrheal diseases. Decreasing the rate of disease in young children, who are more susceptible to severe infections and death, is a top priority. Making these goals a reality, however, will be difficult in light of the challenges (e.g., financial, administrative, cultural) we face in trying to implement key public health practices.

Notes

Chapter 1

1. L. W. Riley et al., "Hemorrhagic Colitis Associated with a Rare *Escherichia coli* Serotype." *New England Journal of Medicine* 308 (1983): 681-685.
2. J. Eberhart-Philips, *Outbreak Alert.* (Oakland, Calif.: New Harbinger Publications, 2000).
3. Ibid.
4. E. Green, "The Bug that Ate the Burger," *Los Angeles Times,* June 6, 2001.
5. B. Van Voris, "Jack in the Box Ends *E. coli* Suits," *The National Law Journal,* November 17, 1997.
6. R. E. Besser et al., "An Outbreak of Diarrhea and Hemolytic Uremic Syndrome from *Escherichia coli* O157:H7 in Fresh-pressed Apple Cider," *Journal of the American Medical Association* 269 (1993): 2217–20.
7. Centers for Disease Control and Prevention, "Outbreaks of *Escherichia coli* O157:H7 Associated with Petting Zoos—North Carolina, Florida, and Arizona, 2004 and 2005," *Morbidity and Mortality Weekly Report* 54 (2005): 1277–80.
8. P. S. Mead et al., "Food-related Illness and Death in the United States," *Emerging Infectious Diseases* 5 (1999): 607–25.
9. S. D. Manning et al., "Variation in Virulence among Clades of *Escherichia coli* O157:H7 Associated with Disease Outbreaks," *Proceedings of the National Academy of the Sciences* 105 (2008): 4868–73.

Chapter 2

1. H. R. Smith and T. Cheasty, "Diarrheal Diseases due to *Escherichia coli* and *Aeromonas,*" *Tapley and Wilson's Microbiology and Microbial Infections,* eds. L. Collier, A. Balows, and M. Sussman (London: Oxford University Press, 1998).
2. S. T. Shulman, H. C. Friedmann, and R. H. Sims, "Theodor Escherich: the First Pediatric Infectious Diseases Physician?" *Clinical Infectious Diseases* 45 (2007): 1025–29.
3. Ibid.

Chapter 3

1. S. Watts, *Epidemics and History: Disease, Power and Imperialism* (New Haven, Conn.: Yale University Press, 1997).
2. G. Rosen, *A History of Public Health* (Baltimore: Johns Hopkins University Press, 1993).
3. M. Bateman and C. McGahey, "A Framework for Action: Child Diarrhea Prevention," *Global Healthlillk* (September 9, 2001).
4. P. H. Dennehy, "Acute Diarrheal Disease in Children: Epidemiology, Prevention, and Treatment," *Infectious Disease Clinics of North America* 19 (2005): 585–602.
5. World Health Organization, "Global Burden of Disease, 2004," http://www.who.int/healthinfo/global_burden_disease/GBD_report_2004update_part2.pdf (accessed March 8, 2010).
6. H. Herikstad et al, "A Population-based Estimate of the Burden of Diarrhoeal Illness in the United States: FoodNet, 1996-7," *Epidemiology and Infection* 129 (2002): 9–17.
7. K. Abbasi, "The World Bank and World Health: Healthcare Strategy," British Medical Journal 318 (1999): 933–36.
8. M. O'Ryan, V. Prado, and L. K. Pickering, "A Millennium Update on Pediatric Diarrheal Illness in the Developing World," *Seminars in Pediatric Infectious Diseases* 16 (2005): 125–36.
9. M. Claeson and M. H. Merson, "Global Progress in the Control of Diarrheal Diseases," *Pediatric Infectious Disease* 9 (1990): 344-355.
10. F. Kauffmann, "The Serology of the coli Group," *Journal of Immunology* 57 (l947): 71–100.
11. I. Orskov et al., "Two New *Escherichia coli* 0 groups: 0172 from Shiga-like Toxin II-Producing Strains (EHEC) and 0173 from Enteroinvasive E. coli (EIEC)," *Acta Pathologica et Microbiologica Scandinavica* 99 (1991): 30–32.
12. Centers for Disease Control and Prevention, National Center for Infectious Diseases, Traveler's Health, "Safe Food

and Water." 2003. http://wwwnc.cdc.gov/travel/content/safe-food-water.aspx (accessed March 8, 2010).

13. R. N. Nguyen et al., "Atypical Enteropathogenic *Escherichia coli* Infection and Prolonged Diarrhea in Children," *Emerging Infectious Diseases* 12 (2006): 597–603.

14. T. J. Ochoa et al., "New Insights into the Epidemiology of Enteropathogenic *Escherichia coli* Infection," *Transactions of the Royal Society of Tropical Medicine and Hygiene* 102 (2008): 852–56; J. P. Nataro et al., "Patterns of Adherence of Diarrheagenic *Escherichia coli* to HEp-2 cells," *Pediatric Infectious Disease Journal* 6 (1987): 829–31.

15. C. Parsot et al., "*Shigella* spp. and Entero-invasive *Escherichia coli* Pathogenicity Factors," *FEMS Microbiology Letters* 252 (2005): 11–18.

Chapter 4

1. R. M. La Ragione, A. Best, M. J. Woodward, and A. D. Wales, "*Escherichia coli* O157:H7 Colonization in Small Domestic Ruminants," *FEMS Microbiology Reviews* 33 (2009): 394–410.

2. R. Cobbold and P. Desmarchelier, "A Longitudinal Study of Shiga-toxigenic *Escherichia coli* (STEC) Prevalence in Three Australian Dairy Herds," *Veterinary Microbiology* 71: 125–37; D. Hancock et al., "The Control of VTEC in the Animal Reservoir," *International Journal of Food Microbiology* 66: 71–8.

3. M. Chase-Topping et al., Super-shedding and the Link between Human Infection and Livestock Carriage of *Escherichia coli* O157," *Nature Reviews Microbiology* 6 (2008): 904–12.

4. D. Hancock et al., "The Control of VTEC in the Animal Reservoir," *International Journal of Food Microbiology* 66 (2001): 71–78.

5. Food Safety and Inspection Service, *Microbiological Results of Raw Ground Beef Products Analylzed for Escherichia coli O157:H7 Calendar Year 2003*, U.S. Department of Agriculture, 2003, http://www.fsis.usda.gov/Science/Ground_Beef_E.Coli_Testing_Results/index.asp (accessed March 8, 2010).

6. D. Hancock et al., "The Control of VTEC in the Animal Reservoir," *International Journal of Food Microbiology* 66: 71–8; J. C. Heaton and K. Jones, "Microbial Contamination of Fruit and Vegetables and the Behaviour of Enteropathogens in the Phyllosphere: A Review," *Journal of Applied Microbiology* 104: 613–26.

7. J. C. Heaton and K. Jones, "Microbial Contamination of Fruit and Vegetables and the Behaviour of Enteropathogens in the Phyllosphere: A Review," *Journal of Applied Microbiology* 104 (2009): 613–26.

8. P. S. Mead et al., "Food-related Illness and Death in the United States," *Emerging Infectious Diseases* 5 (1999): 607–25.

9. R. E. Besser, "An Outbreak of Diarrhea and Hemolytic Uremic Syndrome from *Escherichia coli* O157:H7 in Fresh-Pressed Apple Cider," *Journal of the American Medical Association* 269: 2217–20; S. H. Cody et al., "An Outbreak of *Escherichia coli* O157:H7 Infection from Unpasteurized Commercial Apple Juice," *Annals of Internal Medicine* 130 (1999): 202–9; Centers for Disease Control and Prevention, "*Escherichia coli* O157:H7 Outbreak Linked to Commercially Distributed Dry-cured Salami—Washington and California, 1994," *Morbidity and Mortality Weekly Report* 44 (1995): 157–60; Centers for Disease Control and Prevention, "Multistate Outbreak of *E. coli* O157 Infections, November-December 2006," December 14, 2006, http://www.cdc.gov/ecoli/2006/december/121406.htm; Centers for Disease Control and Prevention, "Ongoing Multistate Outbreak of *Escherichia coli* Serotype O157:H7 Infections Associated with Consumption of Fresh Spinach—United States, September 2006," *Morbidity and Mortality Weekly Report* 55 (2006): 1045–46; T. Breuer et al., "A Multistate Outbreak of *Escherichia coli* O157:H7 Infections Linked to Alfalfa Sprouts Grown from Contaminated Seeds,"

Emerging Infectious Diseases 7 (2001): 977–82; H. Michino et al., "Massive Outbreak of *Escherichia coli* O157:H7 Infection in Schoolchildren in Sakai City, Japan, Associated with Consumption of White Radish Sprouts," *American Journal of Epidemiology* 150 (1999): 787–96; Centers for Disease Control and Prevention, "Outbreak of *Escherichia coli* O157:H7 Infection Associated with Eating Fresh Cheese Curds—Wisconsin, June 1998," *Journal of the American Medical Association* 284 (2000): 2991–2; C. K. Ahn et al., "Deer Sausage: A Newly Identified Vehicle of Transmission of *Escherichia coli* O157: H7," *Journal of Pediatrics* 155, no. 4 (2009): 587–89.

10. J. Tuttle et al., "Lessons from a Large Outbreak of *Escherichia coli* O157: H7 Infections: Insights into the Infectious Dose and Method of Widespread Contamination of Hamburger Patties," *Epidemiology and Infection* 122 (1999): 185–92.

11. R. E. Black et al., "Enterotoxigenic *Escherichia coli* Diarrhoea: Acquired Immunity and Transmission in an Endemic Area," *Bulletin of the World Health Organization* 59 (1981): 263–68.

12. R. E. Fontaine, "Describing the Findings," in *Field Epidemiology,* 2d ed., (New York: Oxford University Press, 2002).

13. S. T. David et al., "Petting Zoo-associated *Escherichia coli* O157:H7—Secondary Transmission, Asymptomatic Infection, and Prolonged Shedding in the Classroom," *Canada Communicable Disease Report* 30 (2004), http://www.phac-aspc.gc.ca/publicat/ccdr-rmtc/04vol30/dr3020a-eng.php.

Chapter 5

1. U.S. Department of Health and Human Services, "Progress Review: Food Safety," http://www.healthypeople.gov/data/2010prog/focus10/default.htm, December 20, 2007.

2. Centers for Disease Control and Prevention, "Preliminary FoodNet Data on the Incidence of Infection with Pathogens Transmitted Commonly through Food—10 states, 2007," *Morbidity and Mortality Weekly Report* 57 (2008): 366–70; E. Scallan, "Activities, Achievements, and Lessons Learned during the First 10 Years of the Foodborne Diseases Active Surveillance Network: 1996–2005," *Clinical Infectious Diseases* 44 (2007): 718–25.

3. Centers for Disease Control and Prevention. "Preliminary FoodNet Data on the Incidence of Infection with Pathogens Transmitted Commonly through Food—10 states, 2007," *Morbidity and Mortality Weekly Report* 57 (2008): 366–70.

4. M. Lynch, J. Painter, R. Woodruff, and C. Braden, "Surveillance for Foodborne-Disease Outbreaks—United States, 1998–2002," *MMWR Surveillance Summaries* 55 (2006): 1–42.

5. See note 3 above.

6. J. T. Brooks et al., "Non-O157 Shiga Toxin-producing *Escherichia coli* Infections in the United States, 1983-2002," *Journal of Infectious Diseases* 192: 1422–29.

7. H. I. Huppertz, "Diarrhea in Young Children Associated with *Escherichia coli* non-O157 Organisms That Produce Shiga-like Toxin," *Journal of Pediatrics* 128: 341–6.

8. K. E. Johnson, C. M. Thorpe, and C. L. Sears, "The Emerging Clinical Importance of Non-O157 Shiga Toxin-producing *Escherichia coli*," *Clinical Infectious Diseases* 43: 1587–95.

9. A. Gerber et al., "Clinical Course and the Role of Shiga Toxin-producing *Escherichia coli* Infection in the Hemolytic-uremic Syndrome in Pediatric Patients, 1997-2000, in Germany and Austria: A Prospective Study," *Journal of Infectious Diseases* 186: 493–500.

10. P. S. Mead et al., "Food-related Illness and Death in the United States," *Emerging Infectious Diseases* 5: 607–25.

11. See note 3 above.

12. P. S. Mead and P. M. Griffin, "*Escherichia coli* O157:H7," *Lancet* 352 (1998): 1207–12.

13. J. M. Rangel et al., "Epidemiology of *Escherichia coli* O157:H7 outbreaks, United States, 1982-2002," *Emerging Infectious Diseases* 11 (2005): 603–9.

14. A. Caprioli, S. Morabito, H. Brugere, and E. Oswald, "Enterohaemorrhagic *Escherichia coli*: Emerging Issues on Virulence and Modes of Transmission," *Veterinary Research* 36 (2005): 289–311.

15. R. M. Robins-Browne, "The Relentless Evolution of Pathogenic *Escherichia coli*," *Clinical Infectious Diseases* 41 (2009): 793–4.

16. M. Rivas et al., "Characterization and Epidemiologic Subtyping of Shiga Toxin-producing *Escherichia coli* Strains Isolated from Hemolytic Uremic Syndrome and Diarrhea Cases in Argentina," *Foodborne Pathogens and Disease* 3 (2006): 88–96.

17. A. Gerber et al., "Clinical Course and the Role of Shiga Toxin-producing *Escherichia coli* Infection in the Hemolytic-uremic Syndrome in Pediatric Patients, 1997-2000, in Germany and Austria: A Prospective Study," *Journal of Infectious Diseases* 186 (2002): 493–500; K. E. Johnson, C. M. Thorpe, and C. L. Sears, "The Emerging Clinical Importance of Non-O157 Shiga Toxin-producing *Escherichia coli*," *Clinical Infectious Diseases* 43 (2006): 1587–95.

18. S. M. Jernigan and F. B. Waldo, "Racial Incidence of Hemolytic Uremic Syndrome," *Pediatric Nephrology* (1994): 545–7; J. P. Haack et al., "*Escherichia coli* O157 Exposure in Wyoming and Seattle: Serologic Evidence of Rural Risk," *Emerging Infectious Diseases* 9 (2003): 1226–31; S. J. O'Brien, G. K. Adak, and C. Gilham, "Contact with Farming Environment as a Major Risk Factor for Shiga Toxin (Vero cyto-toxin)-producing *Escherichia coli* O157 Infection in Humans," *Emerging Infectious Diseases* 7 (2001): 1049–51; P. I. Tarr, C. A. Gordon, and W. L. Chandler,

"Shiga-toxin-producing *Escherichia coli* and Haemolytic Uraemic Syndrome," *Lancet* 365 (2005): 1073–86.

19. P. I. Tarr, C. A. Gordon, and W. L. Chandler, "Shiga-toxin-producing *Escherichia coli* and Haemolytic Uraemic Syndrome," *Lancet* 365 (2005): 1073–86.

20. See note 3 above.

21. J. C. Buzby and T. Roberts, "The Economics of Enteric Infections: Human Foodborne Disease Costs," *Gastroenterology* 136 (2009): 1851-62.

22. T. J. Ochoa, F. Barletta, C. Contreras, and E. Mercado, "New Insights into the Epidemiology of Enteropathogenic *Escherichia coli* Infection," *Transactions of the Royal Society of Tropical Medicine and Hygiene* 102 (2008): 852–6.

23. N. Al-Gallas et al., "Etiology of Acute Diarrhea in Children and Adults in Tunis, Tunisia, with Emphasis on Diarrheagenic *Escherichia coli*: Prevalence, Phenotyping, and Molecular Epidemiology," *American Journal of Tropical Medicine and Hygiene* 77 (2007): 571–82.

24. J. E. Afset, L. Bevanger, P. Romundstad, and K. Bergh, "Association of Atypical Enteropathogenic *Escherichia coli* (EPEC) with Prolonged Diarrhoea," *Journal of Medical Microbiology* 53 (2004): 1137–44; R. N. Nguyen, L. S. Taylor, M. Tauschek, and R. M. Robins-Browne, "Atypical Enteropathogenic *Escherichia coli* Infection and Prolonged Diarrhea in Children," *Emerging Infectious Diseases* 12 (2006): 597–603.

25. T. Estrada-Garcia et al., "Association of Diarrheagenic *Escherichia coli* Pathotypes with Infection and Diarrhea among Mexican Children and Association of Atypical Enteropathogenic *E. coli* with Acute Diarrhea," *Journal of Clinical Microbiology* 47 (2009): 93–98.

26. See note 23 above.

27. M. R. Rao et al., "High Disease Burden of Diarrhea due to Enterotoxigenic *Escherichia coli* among Rural Egyptian Infants and Young Children," *Journal*

of *Clinical Microbiology* 41 (2003): 4862–64.

28. See note 25 above.

29. See note 27 above.

30. F. Qadri, A. M. Svennerholm, A. S. Faruque, and R. B. Sack, "Enterotoxigenic *Escherichia coli* in Developing Countries: Epidemiology, Microbiology, Clinical Features, Treatment, and Prevention," *Clinical Microbiology Reviews* 18 (2005): 465–83.

31. J. P. Nataro, and J. B. Kaper, "Diarrheagenic *Escherichia coli*," *Clinical Microbiology Reviews* 11 (1998): 143–201.

32. D. B. Huang, "Enteroaggregative *Escherichia coli* Is a Cause of Acute Diarrheal Illness: A Meta-analysis, *Clinical Infectious Diseases* 43 (2006): 556–63.

33. G. D. Fang et al., "Etiology and Epidemiology of Persistent Diarrhea in Northeastern Brazil: A Hospital-based, Prospective, Case-control Study," *Journal of Pediatric Gastroenterology and Nutrition* 21 (1995): 137–44; see note 25 above.

34. N. Vieira et al., "High Prevalence of Enteroinvasive *Escherichia coli* Isolated in a Remote Region of Northern Coastal Ecuador," *American Journal of Tropical Medicine and Hygiene* 76 (2007): 528–33.

35. A. Weintraub et al., "Enteroaggregative *Escherichia coli*: Epidemiology, Virulence and Detection," *Journal of Medical Microbiology* 56 (2007): 4–8.

36. W. L. Pabst et al., "Prevalence of Enteroaggregative Escherichia coli among Children With and Without Diarrhea in Switzerland," *Journal of Clinical Microbiology* 41: 2289–93.

37. See note 35 above.

38. E. F. Tulloch Jr., K. J. Ryan, S. B. Formal, and F. A. Franklin, "Invasive Enteropathic *Escherichia coli* Dysentery: An Outbreak in 28 Adults," *Annals of Internal Medicine* 79 (1973): 13–17; M. E. Gordillo et al., "Molecular Characterization of Strains of Enteroinvasive Escherichia coli O143, Including Isolates from a Large Outbreak in Houston,

Texas," *Journal of Clinical Microbiology* 30 (1992): 889–93.

39. M. M. Levine et al., "Epidemiologic Studies of *Escherichia coli* Diarrheal Infections in a Low Socioeconomic Level Peri-urban Community in Santiago, Chile," *American Journal of Epidemiology* 138 (1993): 849–69.

40. L. C. Spano et al., "Age-specific Prevalence of Diffusely Adherent *Escherichia coli* in Brazilian Children with Acute Diarrhoea," *Journal of Medical Microbiology* 57 (2008): 359–63; P. Valentiner-Branth et al., "Cohort Study of Guinean Children: Incidence, Pathogenicity, Conferred Protection, and Attributable Risk for Enteropathogens during the First 2 Years of Life," *Journal of Clinical Microbiology* 41 (2003): 4238–45.

41. J. Zdziarski et al., "Molecular Basis of Commensalism in the Urinary Tract: Low Virulence or Virulence Attenuation?" *Infection and Immunity* 76 (2008): 695–703.

42. B. Foxman and P. Brown, "Epidemiology of Urinary Tract Infections: Transmission and Risk Factors, Incidence, and Costs," *Infectious Disease Clinics of North America* 17 (2003): 227–41.

43. B. Foxman, K. L. Klemstine, and P. D. Brown, "Acute Pyelonephritis in U.S. Hospitals in 1997: Hospitalization and In-hospital Mortality," *Annals of Epidemiology* 13 (2003): 144–50; L. E. Nicolle, D. Friesen, G. K. Harding, and L. L. Roos, "Hospitalization for Acute Pyelonephritis in Manitoba, Canada, during the Period from 1989 to 1992; Impact of Diabetes, Pregnancy, and Aboriginal Origin," *Clinical Infectious Diseases* 22 (1996): 1051–6.

44. B. Foxman, K. L. Klemstine, and P. D. Brown, "Acute Pyelonephritis in U.S. Hospitals in 1997: Hospitalization and In-hospital Mortality," *Annals of Epidemiology* 13 (2003): 144–50.

45. See note 42 above.

46. B. Foxman et al., "Urinary Tract Infection: Self-reported Incidence and Associated

Costs," *Annals of Epidemiology* 10 (2000): 509–15; W. R. Jarvis, "Selected Aspects of the Socioeconomic Impact of Nosocomial Infections: Morbidity, Mortality, Cost, and Prevention," *Infection Control and Hospital Epidemiology* 17 (1996): 552-57; S. Saint, "Clinical and Economic Consequences of Nosocomial Catheter-Related Bacteriuria," *American Journal of Infection Control* (2000): 68-75.

47. S. J. Schrag, "Risk Factors for Invasive, Early-onset *Escherichia coli* Infections in the Era of Widespread Intrapartum Antibiotic Use," *Pediatrics* 118 (2006): 570–76.

48. T. B. Hyde, "Trends in Incidence and Antimicrobial Resistance of Early-onset Sepsis: Population-based Surveillance in San Francisco and Atlanta," *Pediatrics* 110 (2002): 690–5.

49. Ibid.

50. See note 47 above.

Chapter 6

1. J. P. Nataro and J. B. Kaper, "Diarrheagenic *Escherichia coli*," *Clinical Microbiology Reviews* 11 (1998): 142–201.

2. T. M. Bergholz and T. S. Whittam, "Variation in Acid Resistance among Enterohaemorrhagic *Escherichia coli* in a Simulated Gastric Environment," *Journal of Applied Microbiology* 102 (2007): 352–62.

3. See note 1 above.

4. K. Jann and B. Jann, "Polysaccharide Antigens of *Escherichia coli*," *Review of Infectious Disease* 9 Suppl 5 (1987): S517–26.

5. I. Rosenshine et al., "A Pathogenic Bacterium Triggers Epithelial Signals to Form a Functional Bacterial Receptor That Mediates Actin Pseudopod Formation," *EMBO Journal* 15 (1996): 2613–24.

6. See note 1 above.

7. E. Strauch et al., "Bacteriophage 2851 is a Prototype Phage for Dissemination of the Shiga Toxin Variant Gene 2c in E. coli O157:H7," *Infection and Immunity* 76, no. 12 (2008): 5466–77.

8. S. Persson, K. E. Olsen, S. Ethelberg, and F. Scheutz, "Subtyping Method for *Escherichia coli* Shiga Toxin (verocytotoxin) 2 Variants and Correlations to Clinical Manifestations," *Journal of Clinical Microbiology* 45 (2007): 2020–4.

9. A. W. Friedrich et al., "*Escherichia coli* Harboring Shiga Toxin 2 Gene Variants: Frequency and Association with Clinical Symptoms," *Journal of Infectious Diseases* 185 (2002): 74–84; J. K. Jelacic et al., "Shiga Toxin-producing *Escherichia coli* in Montana: Bacterial Genotypes and Clinical Profiles," *Journal of Infectious Diseases* 188 (2003): 719–29.

10. S. D. Manning, et al., "Variation in Virulence among Clades of *Escherichia coli* O157:H7 Associated with Disease Outbreaks," *Proceedings of the National Academy of Sciences* 105 (2008): 4868–73.

11. J. M. Sanger et al., "Novel Form of Actin-based Motility Transports Bacteria on the Surfaces of Infected Cells," *Cell Motility and the Cytoskeleton* 34 (1996): 279–87.

12. M. K. Wolf et al., "Occurrence, Distribution, and Associations of O and H Serogroups, Colonization Factor Antigens, and Toxins of Enterotoxigenic *Escherichia coli*," *Clinical Microbiology Reviews* 10 (1987): 569–84.

13. J. R. Czeczulin et al., "Aggregative Adherence Fimbria II, a Second Fimbrial Antigen Mediating Aggregative Adherence in Enteroaggregative *Escherichia coli*," *Infection and Immunity* 65 (1997): 4135–45; J. P. Nataro et al., "Aggregative Adherence Fimbriae I of Enteroaggregative *Escherichia coli* Mediate Adherence to HEp-2 Cells and Hemagglutination of Human Erythrocytes," *Infection and Immunity* 60 (1992): 2297–304.

14. C. Bernier, P. Gounon, and C. Le Bouguenec, "Identification of an Aggregative Adhesion Fimbria (AAF) Type III-Encoding Operon in Enteroaggregative *Escherichia coli* as a Sensitive Probe for Detecting the AAF-encoding Operon Family," *Infection and Immunity* 70 (2002): 4302–11.

15. See note 1 above.

16. C. Bernier, P. Gounon, and C. Le Bou-
guenec, "Identification of an Aggrega-
tive Adhesion Fimbria (AAF) Type
III-Encoding Operon in Enteroag-
gregative *Escherichia coli* as a Sensitive
Probe for Detecting the AAF-encoding
Operon Family," *Infection and Immunity*
70 (2002): 4302–11; S. J. Savarino et
al., "Enteroaggregative *Escherichia coli*
Heat-stable Enterotoxin 1 Represents
Another Subfamily of *E. coli* Heat-stable
Toxin," *Proceedings of the National
Academy of Sciences* 90: 3093–7.

17. S. J. Savarino et al., "Enteroaggregative
Escherichia coli Heat-stable Enterotoxin
Is Not Restricted to Enteroaggregative
E. coli," *Journal of Infectious Diseases*
173 (1996): 1019–22.

18. A. Allaoui et al., "MxiG, a Membrane
Protein Required for Secretion of Shi-
gella spp. Ipa invasins: Involvement
in Entry into Epithelial Cells and in
Intercellular Dissemination," *Molecular
Microbiology* 17 (1995): 461–70; J. P.
Nataro and J. B. Kaper, "Diarrheagenic
Escherichia coli," *Clinical Microbiology
Reviews* 11 (1998): 142–201.

19. S. W. Pawlowski, C. A. Warren, and R.
Guerrant, "Diagnosis and Treatment of
Acute or Persistent Diarrhea," *Gastroen-
terology* 136 (2009): 1874–86.

20. See note 1 above.

21. M. E. Charbonneau and M. Mourez,
"Functional Organization of the Auto-
transporter Adhesin Involved in Diffuse
Adherence," *Journal of Bacteriology* 189
(2007): 9020–9.

22. S. S. Bilge, C. R. Clausen, W. Lau, and S.
L. Moseley, "Molecular Characterization of a Fimbrial Adhesin, F1845,
Mediating Diffuse Adherence of Diar-
rhea-associated *Escherichia coli* to HEp-
2 Cells," *Journal of Bacteriology* 171
(1989): 4281–89.

23. C. Beinke et al., "Diffusely Adhering
Escherichia coli Strains Induce Attaching
and Effacing Phenotypes and Secrete
Homologs of Esp Proteins," *Infection and
Immunity* 66 (1998): 528–39.

24. See note 1 above.

25. A. L. Servin, "Pathogenesis of Afa/Dr
Diffusely Adhering *Escherichia coli*,"
Clinical Microbiology Reviews 18
(2005): 264–92.

26. T. J. Wiles, R. R. Kulesus, and M. A. Mul-
vey, "Origins and virulence mechanisms
of uropathogenic *Escherichia coli*,"
Experimental and Molecular Pathology
85 (2008): 11–19.

27. B. K. Billips, A. J. Schaeffer, and D. J.
Klumpp, "Molecular Basis of Uropathogenic *Escherichia coli* Evasion of the
Innate Immune Response in the Bladder," *Infection and Immunity* 76 (2008):
3891–900.

28. See note 26 above.

Chapter 7

1. J. P. Nataro and J. B. Kaper, "Diarrheagenic
Escherichia coli," *Clinical Microbiology
Reviews* 11 (1998): 142–201.

2. J. P. Nataro et al., "Patterns of Adherence
of Diarrheagenic *Escherichia coli* to
HEp-2 Cells," *Pediatric Infectious Disease Journal* 6 (1987): 829–31.

3. K. Kimata et al., "Rapid Categorization of
Pathogenic *Escherichia coli* by Multiplex
PCR," *Microbiology and Immunology* 49
(2005): 485–92.

4. See note 1 above.

5. M. M. Aslani et al., "Molecular Detec-
tion and Antimicrobial Resistance of
Diarrheagenic *Escherichia coli* Strains
Isolated from Diarrheal Cases," *Saudi
Medical Journal* 29 (2008): 388–92.

6. T. V. Nguyen, P. V. Le, C. H. Le, and A.
Weintraub, "Antibiotic Resistance in
Diarrheagenic *Escherichia coli* and Shi-
gella Strains Isolated from Children in
Hanoi, Vietnam," *Antimicrobial Agents
and Chemotherapy* 49 (2008): 816–9.

7. S. Gulsun, N. Oguzoglu, A. Inan, and N.
Ceran, "The Virulence Factors and
Antibiotic Sensitivities of *Escherichia
coli* Isolated from Recurrent Urinary
Tract Infections," *Saudi Medical Journal*
26 (2005): 1755–58.

8. M. J. Schwaber et al., "Clinical and Economic Impact of Bacteremia with

Extended-spectrum Beta-lactamase Producing Enterobacteriaceae," *Antimicrobial Agents and Chemotherapy* 50 (2005): 1257–62.

9. J. P. Nataro and J. B. Kaper, "Diarrheagenic *Escherichia coli*," *Clinical Microbiology Reviews* 11 (1998): 142–201; C. Mietens et al., "Treatment of Infantile *E. coli* Gastroenteritis with Specific Bovine Anti-*E. coli* Milk Immunoglobulins," *European Journal of Pediatrics* 132 (1979): 239–52.

Chapter 8

1. U.S. Department of Agriculture, "Food Safety," *Agriculture Fact Book,* http://www.usda.gov/factbook (accessed March 8, 2010).

2. Food Safety and Inspection Service, "FSIS Food Recalls," http://www.fsis.usda.gov/factsheets/FSIS_Food_Recalls/index.asp (accessed October 8, 2009).

3. Food Safety and Inspection Service, "Hudson Foods Recalls Beef Burgers Nationwide for *E. coli* O157:H7," http://www.fsis.usda.gov/OA/recalls/prelease/pr015-97.htm (posted August 12, 1997).

4. Centers for Disease Control and Prevention, "Preliminary FoodNet Data on the Incidence of Infection with Pathogens Transmitted Commonly through Food—10 states, 2007," *Morbidity and Mortality Weekly Report* 57 (2008): 366–70.

5. T. P. Stephens, G. H. Loneragan, E. Karunasena, and M. M. Brashears, "Reduction of *Escherichia coli* O157 and Salmonella in Feces and on Hides of Feedlot Cattle Using Various Doses of a Direct-fed Microbial," *Journal of Food Protection* 70 (2007): 2386–91.

6. D. R. Smith et al., "A Two-dose Regimen of a Vaccine against Type III Secreted Proteins Reduced *Escherichia coli*

O157:H7 Colonization of the Terminal Rectum in Beef Cattle in Commercial Feedlots," *Foodborne Pathogens and Disease* 6 (2009): 155–61; A. B. Thornton et al., "Effects of a Siderophore Receptor and Porin Proteins-based Vaccination on Fecal Shedding of *Escherichia coli* O157:H7 in Experimentally Inoculated Cattle," *Journal of Food Protection* 72 (2009): 866–69.

7. R. P. Johnson et al., "Bacteriophages for Prophylaxis and Therapy in Cattle, Poultry, and Pigs," *Animal Health Research Reviews* 9 (2008): 201–15.

8. J. M. Sargeant, M. R. Amezcua, A. Rajic, and L. Waddell, "Pre-harvest Interventions to Reduce the Shedding of *E. coli* O157 in the Faeces of Weaned Domestic Ruminants: A Systematic Review," *Zoonoses and Public Health* 54 (2007): 260–77.

9. P. Mead and P. M. Griffin, "*Escherichia coli* O157:H7." *Lancet* 352 (1998): 1207-1212.

10. University of Wisconsin–Madison, "Hunting Down A Dangerous Intruder," news release, June 30, 1998, http://news.cals.wisc.edu/newsDisplay.asp?id=808.

Chapter 9

1. A. M. Svennerholm and J. Tobias, "Vaccines Against Enterotoxigenic *Escherichia coli*," *Expert Review of Vaccines* 7 (2008): 795–804.

2. G. D. Armstrong et al., "A Phase I Study of Chemically Synthesized Verotoxin (Shiga-like toxin) Pk-trisaccharide Receptors Attached to Chromosorb for Preventing Hemolytic-uremic Syndrome," *Journal of Infectious Diseases* 171 (1995): 1042–45; J. P. Nataro and J. B. Kaper, "Diarrheagenic *Escherichia coli*," *Clinical Microbiology* 11 (1998): 142–201

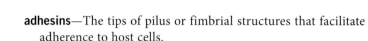

adhesins—The tips of pilus or fimbrial structures that facilitate adherence to host cells.

agar—A substance included in growth media that solidifies to provide an ideal environment for culturing and growing bacteria.

antimicrobial agent—A molecule or substance that can kill or prevent the growth of bacteria. Antibacterial agents can be used to treat patients with specific bacterial infections; antibiotics represent a type of antibacterial agent.

antibiotic—A molecule or substance that can kill or prevent the growth of a microorganism. Antibiotics are used to treat patients with specific bacterial infections.

antibiotic resistance—The ability of a bacterium to develop resistance to the killing effects of certain antibiotics.

antibodies—Proteins that are produced by specialized immune cells (B lymphocytes) that are specific for a foreign substance (antigen). An antibody helps the body eliminate infectious agents via a complex cascade of immune responses.

antigen—A microorganism or product of a microorganism (e.g., the *E. coli* cell wall) that triggers a human immune response.

asymptomatic bacteriuria—A condition in which a person has a high density of bacteria in their urine, but has no symptoms.

asymptomatic colonization—A condition in which a person (host) has a potentially harmful microorganism in their body, but they fail to develop no disease symptoms.

bacterial colonies—A visible cluster of bacteria growing on a solid growth medium (e.g., agar) that are genetically identical because they originated from a single parent cell.

bacteriologist—Scientist who studies single-celled prokaryotic microorganisms called bacteria.

bacteriophages—Viruses that infect bacteria. Some bacteriophages can carry important virulence genes (e.g., Shiga toxins).

bacterium—Single-celled prokaryotic microorganism that lacks a nuclear membrane to hold its genetic material, or DNA. Plural is *bacteria*.

bioterrorism—The use of bacteria, viruses, or the toxins produced by these microorganisms as weapons.

case definition—Refers to the method that public health officials determine what criteria (e.g. symptoms, etc.) classifies individuals as having a specific illness or condition.

cell division—The separation of one cell into two cells (daughter cells).

cell membrane—The structure that envelops a cell.

cell wall—A complex structure located outside the cell membrane of bacteria that acts as a protective barrier. The cell wall differs among gram-negative and gram-positive bacteria.

chronic disease—Medical condition that is often permanent and incurable, and can leave a person permanently disabled. Chronic diseases can be either infectious or noninfectious in origin.

colonization—The establishment of bacteria within a person. Colonization may or may not lead to infection.

colonization factors—Refers to the many distinct types of fimbrae among enterotoxigenic *E. coli* (ETEC).

commensals—Microorganisms that live on or inside a host without causing harm.

cytoplasm—The internal gel-like liquid material inside of a cell.

daughter cell—A cell produced from a single parent cell following cell division. A daughter cell is identical to the parent cell unless a genetic mutation occurs.

deoxyribonucleic acid (DNA)—A double-stranded molecule that encodes the genetic information of a cell.

diarrhea—Frequent loose or liquid stools.

diarrheagenic E. coli—Refers to the group of *E. coli* types that cause diarrheal disease. Common *E. coli* types include EHEC, ETEC, EPEC, DAEC, EAEC, and EIEC.

diarrheal disease—An illness in which the dominant symptom is diarrhea.

endemic disease—The background level of a specific infectious agent or disease that is constantly present in a given population.

endotoxin—A substance present on the surface of gram-negative bacteria that is released when cells are destroyed by infection.

enterohemorrhagic E. coli (EHEC)—*E. coli* strains that produce Shiga toxins and cause severe diarrhea and hemolytic uremic syndrome (HUS) in some people, particulary young children.

epidemic—A sudden increase in the presence of an infectious agent or disease in a population that exceeds the endemic level. Also known as an outbreak.

epidemiology—The study of the occurrence of disease or health-related conditions within a given population.

eukaryote—A cell that contains a nucleus with genetic material surrounded by a defined membrane, as well as other important cellular structures.

facultative anaerobe—A microorganism that can survive either with or without oxygen.

fecal-oral route—Transmission of infectious agents via ingestion of food or water that has been contaminated by feces.

fermentation—The process of generating energy by oxidizing certain organic compounds.

fimbriae—Rigid arm-like appendages that extend from the bacterial cell surface and facilitate attachment to and colonization of human mucous membranes via adherence factors. Fimbriae are common to most *E. coli* strains and are also referred to as pili (*pilus*, singular).

flagella—Tail-like appendages on cells that are responsible for locomotion but not attachment. Singular is *flagellum*.

foodborne disease—An infection or illness caused by a microorganism or toxin that was present in food or water.

fungus—A group of flowerless and seedless plants (e.g., molds, mushrooms, and yeast) that are asexual and reproduce via spores.

gastroenteritis—Inflammation of the stomach and intestinal lining that contributes to nausea, diarrhea, stomach pain, and weakness. Many different infectious agents, including many *E. coli* types, cause gastroenteritis.

gastrointestinal (GI) tract—Organ structures that include the oral cavity, esophagus, stomach, intestines, rectum, and anus.

genitourinary tract—The organs and structures that include the kidneys, ureters, bladder, and urethra.

gram-negative—Refers to the type of bacteria that cannot retain the color of the initial stain following the Gram stain procedure. *E. coli* is a gram-negative organism.

gram-positive—Refers to the type of bacteria that retain the color of the initial stain following the Gram stain procedure.

growth medium—A synthetic substance that contains essential nutrients that enhance the growth of microorganisms for culture in a laboratory.

H-antigen—The antigen in the flagella of motile bacteria.

hemolytic uremic syndrome (HUS)—A rare condition that most often affects young children and may lead to kidney failure and death.

host—An organism that is infected or colonized with a microorganism.

immunocompromised—When a person's immune system is not functioning properly, thereby making the individual more susceptible to infections.

incidence—The rate at which new cases of disease spread among people in a given population during a specific time period.

indole—A biochemical product that is formed following degradation of tryptophan present in a solution. *E. coli* can produce indole, and can be identified based on this biochemical characteristic.

infectious disease—A disease caused by infection with a microorganism such as a virus, bacterium, parasite, or fungus.

infectious dose—The amount of an infectious agent that is required to cause disease in an individual.

lactoferrin—A protein found in milk that has antimicrobial properties.

lipopolysaccharides (LPS)—Polysaccharides containing lipids (fats) that extend out of the bacterial cell wall of gram-negative bacteria (e.g., *E. coli*). The three LPS components determine the bacterial serotype.

MacConkey agar (MAC)—A specific type of growth medium used to identify *E. coli*, which grow in colonies that appear flat, round, and pink.

meningitis—A condition characterized by inflammation of the meninges in the brain.

misclassification bias—This occurs when there is an error in how something is classified, which can make an epidemiological association appear larger or smaller than it really is.

multicellular—Refers to organisms (such as humans) that are composed of many types of cells.

multidrug resistance—The ability of some microorganisms to withstand the killing effects of more than one antibiotic.

mutation—An alteration or change in the genetic material of a cell.

natural selection—Process by which specific traits that enhance survival get passed on to offspring.

normal flora—The millions of microorganisms (microbiota) that normally reside in the human body. They produce essential vitamins and help protect humans from invasion by disease-causing microorganisms. In some cases, however, microbiota members can become pathogens.

nosocomial infection—An infection acquired in a hospital or health care setting.

notifiable disease—Disease or infectious agent that must be reported to a health department or governmental official.

nucleotides—The building blocks of DNA.

nucleus—The major organelle of eukaryotic cells that contains the chromosomes, or genetic material, within an envelope.

O-antigen—The somatic antigen of gram-negative bacteria that makes up the cell wall or lipopoly saccharide.

opportunistic infections—Infections caused by a microorganism that does not normally cause disease, but only does so in certain situations (e.g., in immunocompromised people).

outbreak—A sudden increase in disease frequency in a given population. Also known as an epidemic.

outer membrane—Part of the bacterial cell wall that is composed of proteins and fatty acids.

pandemic—An epidemic that occurs in multiple countries within a particular period of time.

parasite—An organism (e.g., *Giardia lamblia*) that obtains food and shelter from another organism (e.g., a human).

pathogen—A microorganism known to cause disease.

pathogenesis—The process by which a pathogen causes disease.

pathogenicity island—A class or set of genes that often contain important virulence genes and can be readily transferred between bacteria.

phospholipids—Lipids, or fatty acid substances, found in all living cells and in the bilayers of cell membranes.

phylogenetic lineage—An evoluationarily related group with similar genetic characteristics.

pili—Arm-like appendages that facilitate attachment to host cells. Also referred to as *fimbriae.*

plasmid—A small independent piece of chromosomal DNA that is capable of making copies of itself and has the ability to transfer between bacteria. Plasmids often carry virulence and antibiotic resistance genes.

polymerase chain reaction (PCR)—A molecular technique that enables researchers to assess whether specific DNA sequences (e.g., those specific to *E. coli* toxin genes) are present in a laboratory specimen.

polysaccharide—A chain of simple sugar molecules (monosaccharides) that are present in the capsule of certain bacteria.

prevalence—The number of people in a population who have a specific disease or infectious agent divided by the total number of people in the population.

probiotics—Bacteria that have a beneficial effect when introduced into a human host, which typically occurs via food.

prokaryote—A unicellular microorganism that has genetic material flowing freely inside the cell rather than enclosed within a nucleus.

pulsed-field gel electrophoresis (PFGE)—A molecular technique that creates a unique DNA fingerprint, or banding pattern, for each bacterial strain tested. The technique is useful for investigating foodborne disease outbreaks.

reference laboratory—A government-operated laboratory that provides support for other institutions, such as hospitals and health-care clinics, that do not have the ability or finances to evaluate laboratory specimens properly.

reservoir—An organism (e.g., human) or environment (e.g., water) that harbors a pathogenic infectious agent that can be transmitted to other organisms.

restriction enzyme—A digestive enzyme that leaves DNA at specific sites so that DNA fragment sizes can be visualized. This is commonly used to develop DNA fingerprints.

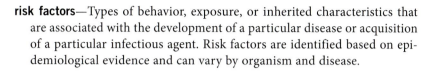

risk factors—Types of behavior, exposure, or inherited characteristics that are associated with the development of a particular disease or acquisition of a particular infectious agent. Risk factors are identified based on epidemiological evidence and can vary by organism and disease.

sepsis—Refers to a condition in which bacteria have infected the blood.

serotype—The form of polysaccharide capsule found in specific bacterial types. Serotyping is a tool used to distinguish between bacterial strains.

Shiga toxin—A potent toxin produced by enterohemorrhagic *E. coli* (EHEC) that is released into intestinal tissue and can contribute to kidney failure.

sorbitol—A type of sugar that is used in growth media to detect the presence of some bacterial types (e.g., *E. coli* O157:H7). Bacteria vary in ability to metabolize sorbitol.

specimen—A sample (e.g., blood or urine) taken from a diseased individual that is submitted to a laboratory for testing.

sporadic—Refers to a disease or infectious agent that occurs randomly in an isolated manner and is not part of an outbreak or epidemic.

strain—A specific group with its own characteristics.

subculture—To transfer cells, such as bacteria, to a solid medium (e.g., growth medium with agar) so that they can be visualized and analyzed.

surveillance system—A network relying on the interactions of numerous people that is used to monitor or survey the occurrence of disease or infectious agents in a given population. Systems can be either active or passive.

unicellular—Refers to a microorganism that comprises only one cell (e.g., a bacterium).

uropathogenic *E. coli* (UPEC)—A type of *E. coli* that commonly causes urinary tract infections or pyelonephritis, a severe kidney infection.

vaccine—Administration of an infectious agent or component of the agent to a human in order to stimulate an immune response without causing disease. Stimulation of the immune response will lead to immunity, or resistance to future infections by the same agent.

vacuole—A cavity inside a cell that is surrounded by the cell membrane. Some bacteria are capable of surviving inside vacuoles and avoid immune system recognition.

virulence—The capacity of an organism to produce disease after infection.

virulence factors—Characteristics of infectious agents that contribute to disease development.

virulence genes—Genes that encode virulence factors, or pathogen characteristics that are important for disease pathogenesis.

virus—Intracellular parasite that relies on a host for replication and survival. Viruses are comprised of either RNA or DNA, and a protein coat.

Further Resources

Books and Articles

Abbasi, K. "The World Bank and World Health: Healthcare Strategy." *British Medical Journal* 318 (1999): 933–936.

Adam, A. "Biology of Colon Bacillus Dyspepsia and its Relation to Pathogenesis and to Intoxication." *Jahrb Kinderberth* 101 (1923): 295.

Baqui, A. H., R. E. Black, R. B. Sack, et al. "Epidemiological and Clinical Characteristics of Acute and Persistent Diarrhea in Rural Bangladeshi Children." *Acta Paediatrica* 381 (Suppl.) (1992): 15–21.

Bateman, M., and C. McGahey. "A Framework for Action: Child Diarrhea Prevention." *Global Healthlink* (September 9, 2001).

Black, R. E. "Diarrheal Diseases." *Infectious Disease Epidemiology: Theory and Practice*, eds. K. E. Nelson, C. M. Williams, and N.M.H. Graham. Gaithersburg, MD: Aspen Publishers, Inc., 2001.

Black, R. E., K. H. Brown, et al. "Longitudinal Studies of Infectious Diseases and Physical Growth of Children in Rural Bangladesh. II. Incidence of Diarrhea and Association with Known Pathogens." *American Journal of Epidemiology* 115 (1982): 315–324.

Bray, J. "Isolation of Antigenically Homogeneous Strains of Bact coli neapolitanum from Summer Diarrhoea in Infants." *Journal of Pathology and Bacteriology* 57 (1945): 239–247.

Brown, J. C. *What the heck is penicillin?* 2001. Available online at *http://www.people.ku.edu/~jbrown/penicillin.html*.

Centers for Disease Control and Prevention. *EXCITE: Epidemiology in the Classroom*. National Center for Chronic Disease Prevention and Health Promotion, 2002. Available online at *http://www.cdc.gov/excite/classroom/outbreak_objectives.htm*.

———. "Preliminary FoodNet data on the incidence of foodborne illnesses—Selected sites, United States, 2002." *Morbidity and Mortality Weekly Report* 52 (15) (2003): 340–343.

———. "Summary of Notifiable Diseases—United States, 2000." *Morbidity and Mortality Weekly Report* 49 (2002): 1–102.

———. *What Is PulseNet?* 2003. Available online at *http://www.cdc.gov/pulsenet/what_is.htm*.

Centers for Disease Control and Prevention, National Center for Infectious Diseases. *Traveler's Health: Safe Food and Water*, 2003. Available online at *http://www.cdc.gov/travel/foodwater.htm*.

Claeson, M., and M. H. Merson. "Global Progress in the Control of Diarrheal Diseases." *Pediatric Infectious Disease Journal* 9 (1990): 345–355.

Consumers Union of the United States, Inc. *From Moo to You.* 1999–2003. Available online at *http://www.consumerreports.org.*

Dargatz, D. A., S. J. Wells, L. A. Thomas, et al. "Factors Associated with the Presence of *Escherichia coli* O157:H7 in Feces of Feedlot Cattle." *Journal of Food Protection* 60 (1997): 466–470.

Diez-Gonzalez, F., T. R. Callaway, M. G. Kizoulis, et al. "The Role of Grain Feeding in the Dissemination of Acid-Resistant Escherichia coli from Cattle." Agricultural Research Service, 1998. Available online at *http://warp.nal.usda.gov.*

Dyke, J. Personal communication, 2003.

Eberhart-Philips, J. *Outbreak Alert.* Oakland, CA: New Harbinger Publications, Inc., 2000.

Elder, R. O., J. F. Keen, G. R. Siragusa, et al. "Correlation of Enterhemorrhagic *Escherichia coli* O157:H7 Prevalence in Feces, Hides, and Carcasses of Beef Cattle During Processing." *Proceedings of the National Academy of Sciences USA* 97 (2000): 2999–3003.

Fang, G. D., A.A.M. Lima, C. V. Martins, et al. "Etiology and Epidemiology of Persistent Diarrhea in Northeastern Brazil: A Hospital-Based, Prospective, Case-Control Study." *Journal of Pediatric Gastroenterology and Nutrition* 21 (1995): 137–144.

Fenner, F., A. J. Hall, and W. R. Dowdle. "What is eradication?" *The Eradication of Infectious Diseases*, eds. W. R. Dowdle and D. R. Hopkins. West Sussex, England: John Wiley, 1998.

Food and Drug Administration. FDA News. "Lactoferrin Considered Safe to Fight *E. coli.*" 2003. Available online at *http://www.fda.gov.*

Food Safety and Inspection Service. "Biosecurity and the Food Supply." 2002. Available online at *http://www.fsis.usda.gov/OA/background/biosecurity.htm.*

———. "FSIS Food Recalls." 2002. Available online at *http://www.fsis.usda.gov/OA/background/bkrecalls.htm.*

——— . "Hudson Foods Recalls Beef Burgers Nationwide for *E. coli* O157:H7." 1997. Available online at *http://www.fsis.usda.gov/oa/recalls/prelease/pr015-97.htm.*

————. *Microbiological Results of Raw Ground Beef Products Analyzed for Escherichia coli O157:H7 Calendar Year 2003*. United States Department of Agriculture, 2003. Available online at *http://www.fsis.usda.gov/OPHS/ecoltest/ecpositives.htm*.

————. Office of Policy, Program Development, and Evaluation. "Farm-to-Table Food Safety." Available online at *http://www.fsis.usda.gov/oppde/fslgrs/farm.htm*.

————. Recall Release. "Oregon Firm Recalls Ground Beef Products for Possible *E. coli* O157:H7." 2003. Available online at *http://www.fsis.usda.gov/OA/recalls/prelease/pr021-2003.htm*.

Foxman, B., and P. Brown. "Epidemiology of Urinary Tract Infections: Transmission and Risk Factors, Incidence, and Costs." *Infectious Disease Clinics of North America* 17 (2003): 227–241.

Foxman, B., R. Barlow, H. d'Arcy et al. "Urinary Tract Infection: Estimated Incidence and Associated Costs." *Annals of Epidemiology* 10 (2000): 509–515.

Foxman, B., S. D. Manning, P. Tallman, et al. "Uropathogenic *Escherichia coli* Are More Likely than Commensal *E. coli* To Be Shared Between Heterosexual Sex Partners." *American Journal of Epidemiology* 156 (2002): 1133–1140.

Gallep, G. "Hunting Down a Dangerous Intruder." *Science Report*. University of Wisconsin-Madison College of Agricultural and Life Sciences, 1998.

Gannon, J. C. *The Global Infectious Disease Threat and its Implications for the United States*. National Intelligence Council, 2000. Available online at *http://www.cia.gov/cia/reports/nie/report/nie99-17d.html*.

Gateway to Government Food Safety Information. "Consumer Advice on Disaster Assistance." 2003. Available online at *http://www.foodsafety.gov/~fsg/fsgdisas.html*.

Gibbons, N. E., and R.G.E. Murray. "Proposals Concerning the Higher Taxa of Bacteria." *International Journal of Systemic Bacteriology* 28 (1978): 1–6.

Giles, C., and G. Sangster. "An Outbreak of Infantile Gastro-enteritis in Aberdeen. The Association of a Special Type of Bact. coli with the Infection." *Journal of Hygiene* 46 (1948): 1–9.

Gordillo, M. E., G. R. Reeve, J. Pappas, et al. "Molecular Characterization of Strains of Enteroinvasive *Escherichia coli* O143, Including Isolates from a Large Outbreak in Houston, Texas." *Journal of Clinical Microbiology* 30 (1992): 889–893.

Graunt, J. *Natural and Political Observations Made upon the Bills of Mortality: London, 1662.* Baltimore: Johns Hopkins University Press, 1939.

Green, E. "The Bug that Ate the Burger." *Los Angeles Times*, June 6, 2001.

Griffin, P. M., and R. V. Tauxe. "The Epidemiology of Infections Caused by Escherichia coli O157:H7, Other Enterohemorrhagic *E. coli* and the Associated Hemolytic Uremic Syndrome." *Epidemiologic Reviews* 13 (1991): 60–98.

Hancock, D. D., T. E. Besser, D. H. Rice, et al. "Longitudinal Study of *Escherichia coli* O157:H7 in Fourteen Cattle Herds." *Epidemiology and Infection* 118 (1997): 193–195.

Hennekens, C. H., and J. E. Buring. *Epidemiology in Medicine.* Boston/ Toronto: Little Brown, 1987.

Hippocrates. "On Airs, Waters, and Places." *Medical Classics*, vol. 3, 1938.

Hooten, T. M., A. E. Stapleton, P. Roberts, et al. "Perineal Anatomy and Urine-Voiding Characteristics of Young Men and Women with and without Recurrent Urinary Tract Infections." *Clinical Infectious Diseases* 29 (1999): 1600–1601.

Jarvis, W. R. "Selected Aspects of the Socioeconomic Impact of Nosocomial Infections: Morbidity, Mortality, Cost, and Prevention." *Infection Control and Hospital Epidemiology* 17 (1996): 552–557.

Kauffmann, F. "The Serology of the coli Group." *Journal of Immunology* 57 (1947): 71–100.

March, S. B., and S. Ratnam. "Sorbitol-MacConkey Medium for Detection of *Escherichia coli* O157:H7 Associated with Hemorrhagic Colitis." *Journal of Clinical Microbiology* 23 (1986): 869–872.

Mazzulli, T. "Resistance Trends in Urinary Tract Pathogens and Impact on Management." *Journal of Urology* 168 (2002): 1720–1722.

McGinn, A. P. "The Resurgence of Infectious Diseases." *Epidemic! The World of Infectious Disease*, ed. R. DeSalle. New York: The New Press, 1999.

Mead, P. S., and P. M. Griffin. "*Escherichia coli* O157:H7." *Lancet* 352 (1998): 1207–1212.

Mechie, S. C., P. A. Chapman, and C. A. Siddons. "A Fifteen-Month Study of *Escherichia coli* O157:H7 in a Dairy Herd." *Epidemiology and Infection* 118 (1997): 17–25.

Miller, V. "Good Bacteria Look Promising for Reducing *E. coli.*" *Research Nebraska.* Lincoln: University of Nebraska-Lincoln, 2002.

Moon, H. W., S. C. Whipp, R. A. Argenzio, et al. "Attaching and Effacing Activities of Rabbit and Human Enteropathogenic *Escherichia coli* in Pig and Rabbit Intestines." *Infection and Immunity* 41 (1983).

Murray, C., and A. Lopez. *Global Health Statistics, Vol. 2.* World Health Organization, World Bank, and Harvard School of Public Health, 1996.

Murray, R.G.E. *Fine Structure and Taxonomy of Bacteria, Microbial Classification.* Cambridge: Cambridge University Press, 1962.

Nataro, J. P., and J. B. Kaper. "Diarrheagenic *Escherichia coli.*" *Clinical Microbiology Reviews* 11 (1998): 142–201.

Ørskov I., I. K. Wachsmuth, et al. "Two New *Escherichia coli* O groups: O172 from Shiga-like Toxin II-Producing Strains (EHEC) and O173 from Enteroinvasive *E. coli* (EIEC)." *Acta pathologica et microbiologica Scandinavica* 99 (1991): 30–32.

Paton, J. C., and A. W. Paton. "Methods for Detection of STEC in Humans." *Methods in Molecular Medicine: E. coli: Shiga Toxin Methods and Protocols,* eds. D Philpott and F. Ebel. Totowa, NJ: Humana Press, Inc., 2003.

Paustian, T. University of Wisconsin-Madison, 2003. Available online at *http://www.bact.wisc.edu/MicrotextBook/BacterialStructure/MoreCellWall.html.*

Ramel, G. Earth-Life Web Productions, 2003. Available online at *http://www.earthlife.net/cells.html.*

Riley, L. W., R. S. Remis, S. D. Helgerson, et al. "Hemorrhagic colitis associated with a rare Escherichia coli serotype." *New England Journal of Medicine* 308 (1983): 681–685.

Rosen, G. *A History of Public Health.* Baltimore: Johns Hopkins University Press, 1993.

Saint, S. "Clinical and Economic Consequences of Nosocomial Catheter-Related Bacteriuria." *American Journal of Infection Control* 28 (2000): 68–75.

Sanchez, S., M. D. Lee, B. G. Harmon, et al. "Animal Issues Associated with *Escherichia coli* O157:H7." *Journal of the American Veterinary Medical Association* 221 (2002): 1122–1126.

Schindler, L., D. Kerrigan, and J. Kelly. *Science Behind the News: Understanding the Immune System.* National Cancer Institute, 2003. Available online at *http://press2.nci.nih.gov/sciencebehind/immune/immune08.htm.*

Shea, K. M. "Antibiotic Resistance: What Is the Impact of Agricultural Uses of Antibiotics on Children's Health?" *Pediatrics* 112 (2003): 253–258.

Smith, H. R., and T. Cheasty. "Diarrhoeal Diseases due to *Escherichia coli* and *Aeromonas*." *Topley and Wilson's Microbiology and Microbial Infections*, eds. L. Collier, A. Balows, and M. Sussman. London: Oxford University Press, 1998.

Smith, J. "The Association of Certain Types (alpha and beta) of Bact. coli with Infantile Gastroenteritis." *Journal of Hygiene* 47 (1949): 221–226.

Soper, G. A. "The Curious Case of Typhoid Mary." *Academic Medicine: Journal of the Association of American Medical Colleges* 15 (1939): 698–712.

Stanier, R. Y., and C. B. van Niel. "The Main Outlines of Bacterial Classification." *Journal of Bacteriology* 42 (1941): 437–466.

Teale, C. *Veterinary Surveillance for Antimicrobial Resistance in Campylobacter, Enterococci and Other Bacteria*. Veterinary Laboratories Agency Shrewsbury, 2003. Available online at *http://www.defra.gov.uk/animalh/diseases/zoonoses/conference/ctealeppt.htm*.

Tulloch, A. R., K. J. Ryan, S. B. Formal, and F. A. Franklin. "Invasive enteropathic *Escherichia coli* dysentery." *Annals of Internal Medicine* 79 (1973): 13–17.

United States Department of Agriculture. "Food Safety." *Agriculture Fact Book*. Washington, D.C.: U.S. Government Printing Office, 2002. Available online at *http://www.usda.gov*.

United States Department of Health and Human Services, Centers for Disease Control and Prevention, Office of Communication, Division of Media Relations. 2003. Available online at *http://www.cdc.gov/od/oc/media/pressrel/r030717a.htm*.

United States National Center for Health Statistics. National Vital Statistics Report, vol 51 (5), March 14, 2003. Available online at *http://www.cdc.giv.nchs*.

University of Arizona. "Prokaryotes, Eukaryotes, & Viruses Tutorial." *The Biology Project*, 1999. Available online at *http://www.biology.arizona.edu/cell_bio/tutorials/pev/page1.html*.

Van Voris, B. "Jack in the Box ends *E. coli* suits." *The National Law Journal*. November 17, 1997.

Wanger, A. R., B. E. Murray, P. Echeverria, J. Mathewson, and H. L. DuPont. "Enteroinvasive Escherichia coli in travelers with diarrhea." *Journal of Infectious Diseases* 158 (1988): 640–642.

Watanabe, Y., K. Ozasa, J. H. Mermin, et al. "Factory Outbreak of Escherichia coli O157:H7 Infection in Japan." *Emerging Infectious Diseases* 5 (1999): 424–428.

Watts, S. *Epidemics and History: Disease, Power and Imperialism*. New Haven, CT: Yale University Press, 1997.

WGBH Educational Foundation. *A Science Odyssey: Alexander Fleming*. 1998. Available online at *http://www.pbs.org/wgbh/aso/databank/entries/bmflem.html*.

———. *A Science Odyssey: Fleming Discovers Penicillin*. 1998. Available online at *http://www.pbs.org/wgbh/aso/databank/entries/dm28pe.html*.

Whittam, T. S., E. A. McGraw, and S. D. Reid. "Pathogenic *Escherichia coli* O157: H7: A model for Emerging Infectious Diseases." *Emerging Infections: Biomedical Research Reports*, ed. R. M. Krause. New York: Academic Press, 1998.

World Health Organization. *Food safety and foodborne illness: Fact sheet N237*. World Health Organization, 2002. Available online at *http://www.who.int/mediacentre/factsheets/fs237/en/*.

———. *Reducing Mortality from Major Killers of Children*. 2003. Available online at *http://www.who.int/mediacentre/factsheets/fs178/en/*.

Web Sites

Cells Alive!
http://www.cellsalive.com

Cellular Biology
http://www.biology.arizona.edu/cellbio/tutorials/pev/page1.html

Centers for Disease Control and Prevention (CDC)
http://www.cdc.gov/

E. coli Index
http://web.bham.ac.uk/bcm4ght6/res.html

EXCITE: An Introduction to Epidemiology
http://www.cdc.gov/excite/classroom/intro_epi.htm

EXCITE: How to Investigate an Outbreak
http://www.cdc.gov/excite/classroom/outbreak.htm

National Food Safety Education Month
Partnership for Food Safety Education
http://www.foodsafety.gov/~fsg/september.html

Overview of Infectious Diseases, United States
Central Intelligence Agency (CIA)
http://www.cia.gov/cia/reports/nie/report/nie99-17d.html

PulseNet, Centers for Disease Control and Prevention (CDC)
http://www.cdc.gov/pulsenet/what_is.htm

Summary of Notifiable Diseases,
Centers for Disease Control and Prevention (CDC)
http://www.cdc.gov/mmwr/preview/mmwrhtml/mm4953a1.htm

Understanding the Immune System, National Cancer Institute
http://press2.nci.nih.gov/sciencebehind/immune/immune00.htm

United States Department of Agriculture,
Food Safety and Inspection Service
http://www.fsis.usda.gov/

World Health Organization (WHO)
http://www.who.int

active surveillance systems, 46
adherence, of EPEC, 67–68
AFDO (Association of Food and Drug Officials), 94
agglutination tests, 75, 77
aggregative adherence fimbriae, 69
agriculture industry, 87–94
AIDA-I, 70
AIDS, anti-infective drugs for, 7
aLF Ventures, 97
Animalia, 18
animals, 12–14, 37–38, 82. See also cattle
antibiotic resistance, 81–82
antibiotic-resistant E. coli, 61, 89–90
antibiotic treatment, 81, 89–90
anti-infective drugs, 7
antimicrobials, 97–98
apple cider, 11–12
apple juice, 11–12
Archaebacteria, 18
Association of Food and Drug Officials (AFDO), 94
asymptomatic bacteriuria, 43
asymptomatic colonization, 35
attaching and effacing lesions, 65–67, 68
atypical EPEC, 32, 56–57, 68
avian influenza A (H5N1), 6

bacteria (bacterium), 16, 18, 20–25, 63, 88, 89
bacterial colonies, 73
bacterial culture, 73–75, 76, 79
bacterial infections, 7. See also infectious disease
bacterial sepsis, 34, 43, 60–61, 81
bacteriophages, 67, 88–89
bacteriuria, asymptomatic, 43
beneficial bacteria, 88, 89
biochemical characterization, 75
bioterrorism, 98
bismuth subsalicylate, 83
Bovine Spongiform Encephalopathy (BSE), 6
bundle-forming pilus, 67–68

Campylobacter infections, frequency of, 48
capsular polysaccharides, 64
case definition, for hemolytic uremic syndrome, 54
case investigations, 84
cattle, E. coli in
    E. coli O157:H7, 37
    fecal shedding of, 37, 88, 89
    non-O157 EHEC, 31, 37
    outbreak from, 12–14
    prevention strategies for, 87–90
    in transmission cycle, 42
    transmission of, 37–38
    from water supply, 90–94
causative risk factors, 45
CDC. See Centers for Disease Control and Prevention
cell division, 24
cell wall, 23, 25
Centers for Disease Control and Prevention (CDC), 9, 47, 49
children
    DAEC infections in, 59
    diarrheal disease in, 27, 29
    EAEC infections in, 58
    EIEC infections in, 33
    EPEC infections in, 56
    ETEC infection in, 32, 57
    hemolytic uremic syndrome in, incidence rate of, 54
    incidence of infection in, 49, 99
    newborns, 34, 43, 60–61
    opportunistic infections in, 34
    secondary infection of, 40
cholera, and diarrheal disease, 45
chronic diseases, definition of, 26
cider, E. coli outbreak from, 11–12
colonization
    definition of, 35
    of E. coli
        in animals, 37–38
        asymptomatic, 35
        attaching and effacing lesions in, 65–67, 68

diarrheagenic *E. coli,* 36, 62–63
in humans, 35–37
in mucosal membranes, 63
pathogenic *E. coli,* 36–37
in pregnant women, 43
prevention of, 87–90
uropathogenic *E. coli* (UPEC),
36
colonization factors, 68
commensal bacteria, 16
Communicable Disease Center (CDC),
9
communicable diseases, deaths and
disabilities from, 6
compost, *E. coli* contamination by, 39
consumers, in disease prevention, 94
Creutzfeldt-Jakob disease, human variant (vCJD), 6
cross-contamination, 91–92
Cryptosporidium infections, frequency
of, 48
culture media, 73
Cyclospora infections, frequency of,
48
cyslitis, 71
cytoplasm, 18, 20–24
cytotoxins, 69

DAEC. *See* diffuse adhering *E. coli*
daughter cell, 24
deaths, 6, 27, 28, 29, 32, 40, 99
decay accelerating factor (DAF), 70
dehydration, from diarrhea, 27
deoxyribonucleic acid (DNA), 24,
50–51, 55
Department of Health and Human
Services, 47
developing countries
antibiotic resistance in, 83
atypical EPEC infections in, 32
communicable diseases in, 6
diarrheal disease in, 27
drinking water in, 94
EAEC infections in, 58

EPEC infections in, 32, 56
ETEC infections in, 32, 57
diagnosis, 72–81
bacterial culture in, 73–75, 76
biochemical characterization in, 75
cellular adherence patterns in,
77–78
enzyme immunoassays in, 78, 80
reference laboratories in, 74
serotyping in, 75–76, 77
of uropathogenic *E. coli* (UPEC),
79–81
virulence gene screening in, 78–79
diarrheagenic *E. coli,* 30–31. *See also*
enteroadherent *E. coli;* enterohemorrhagic *E. coli;* enteroinvasive
E. coli; enteropathogenic *E. coli;*
enterotoxigenic *E. coli*
antibiotic resistance of, 82
colonization of, 36
diagnosis of, 72–81
bacterial culture in, 73–75, 76
biochemical characterization
in, 75
cellular adherence patterns in,
77–78
enzyme immunoassays in, 78, 80
reference laboratories in, 74
serotyping in, 75–76, 77
virulence gene screening in,
78–79
foodborne, U.S. outbreaks of, 49
mechanisms of infection of, 62–65
pathogenesis of, 62
secondary transmission of, 40–41
serotypes of, 30–31, 64
transmission of, 39–41
treatment of, 81–83
diarrheal disease, 27, 28–30, 32, 40,
45, 99
diffuse adhering *E. coli* (DAEC), 59,
66, 70, 77–78, 81
disabilities, from communicable
diseases, 6

disease eradication, 44–45
disease prevention, 47
DNA (deoxyribonucleic acid), 24, 50–51, 55
Dr adhesins, 70

EAEC. *See* enteroadherent *E. coli*
EAF (EPEC adherence factor) plasmid, 68
EAST1 toxin, 69
Ebola virus, 6
E. coli (Escherichia coli)
   about, 16–25
   antibiotic resistance of, 82–83, 89–90
   antimicrobials for, 97–98
   colonization of. *See* colonization
   as commensal, 16
   detection methods for, 97. *See also* diagnosis
   diagnosis of, 72–81
      bacterial culture in, 73–75, 76
      biochemical characterization in, 75
      cellular adherence patterns in, 77–78
      enzyme immunoassays in, 78, 80
      reference laboratories in, 74
      serotyping in, 75–76, 77
      virulence gene screening in, 78–79
   diarrheagenic. *See* diarrheagenic *E. coli*
   discovery of, 16–20
   under electron microscope, 21
   epidemiology of, 44–61
   evolution of, 65, 98
   fecal shedding of, in cattle, 37, 88, 89
   Gram staining of, 22
   mechanisms of infection, 62–65
   multidrug resistance of, 82
   non-diarrheal infections from, 33
   non-O157 EHEC, 31, 37, 53
   in normal flora, 35–36
   outbreaks of, 8–15
   pathogenesis of, 62–71
   prevention of, 84–94, 99
   serotypes of, 63–64
   structure of, 20–25, 63, 64
   transmission of. *See* transmission
   treatment of, 81–83
   types of, 15
E. coli O111:H8 genotype, 31
E. coli O118:H16 genotype, 31
E. coli O157:H7. *See also* enterohemorrhagic *E. coli*
   antibiotic resistance of, 82, 89–90
   as bioterrorism agent, 98
   in cattle, 12–14, 37, 88–90
   culturing, 73–75
   emerging strains of, 14
   epidemic curve for, 40–41
   epidemiology of, 53–54
   in food supply, 8–14, 38, 39, 87
   genotype of, 31
   hemolytic uremic syndrome from, 26, 54–56
   incidence rate of, 51–54, 99
   infections by, 31
   inspection for, 85
   outbreaks of, 8–15
      from food, 8–14, 38, 39
      from petting farms, 12–14
      tracking, 51
      from water, 14, 38–39
      by year and location, 13
   prevalence of, 14
   prevention of, 84
   recalls for, 85–86
   research on, 95
   reservoirs of, 12, 42
   risk factors for, 55
   serotypes of, 30–31
   Shiga toxin from, 31, 45
   sorbitol fermentation by, 73–75
   transmission of, 39, 40–41, 42
   in water supply, 14, 38–39, 90–94

E. coli O26:H11 genotype, 31
E. coli O55:H7, 65
economies, effect of communicable diseases on, 6
edible vaccines, 95–96
education, in *E. coli* prevention, 90
efflux pumps, 82
EHEC. *See* enterohemorrhagic *E. coli*
EIEC. *See* enteroinvasive *E. coli*
EIS (Epidemic Intelligence Service), 9
emerging infections, 6
endotoxins, 25
enteritis, from *E. coli,* 16
enteroadherent *E. coli* (enteroaggregative *E. coli*) (EAEC), 15
   cellular adherence patterns of, 77–78
   as diarrheagenic *E. coli,* 30
   foodborne, U.S. outbreaks of, 49
   incidence rate of, 58–59
   infections by, 32–33
   outbreaks of, 58
   pathogenesis of, 66, 68–69
   risk factors for, 58–59
   surveillance systems for, 58–59
   treatment of, 81
Enterobacteriaceae family, 20
enterohemorrhagic *E. coli* (EHEC), 15, 31. *See also* Shiga toxin
   acid resistance of, 63
   in agriculture industry, 87–94
   antibiotic resistance of, 82
   antimicrobials for, 98
   as bioterrorism agent, 98
   in cattle, 37–38, 87–90
   diagnosing, 78, 79, 80
   as diarrheagenic *E. coli,* 30
   foodborne, U.S. outbreaks of, 49
   genotypes of, 31
   incidence rate of, 51–54
   multidrug resistance of, 82
   outbreaks of, tracking, 51
   pathogenesis of, 65–67

prevention efforts for, 84, 85–87, 95
   research on, 95
   risk factors for, 53
   strains of, 67
   surveillance systems for, 51–54
   transmission of, 37–38, 39, 53
   treatment of, 81
   virulence of, 63
enteroinvasive *E. coli* (EIEC), 15, 30, 33, 58–59, 66, 69, 81
enteropathogenic *E. coli* (EPEC), 15
   adherence of, 67–68
   atypical, 32, 56–57
   bovine milk antibodies for, 83
   in cattle, 37
   cellular adherence patterns of, 77–78
   as diarrheagenic *E. coli,* 30
   incidence rate of, 56–57
   infections by, 32
   pathogenesis of, 66, 67–68
   risk factors for, 56
   surveillance systems for, 56–57
   treatment of, 81
enterotoxigenic *E. coli* (ETEC), 15
   in cattle, 37
   colonization factors of, 68
   diarrhea from, 30
   foodborne, U.S. outbreaks of, 49
   incidence rate of, 57
   infections from, 31–32
   pathogenesis of, 66, 68
   risk factors for, 57
   surveillance systems for, 57
   transmission of, 39–40
   treatment of, 81
   vaccine against, 95, 97
   virulence of, 63
environmental risk factors, 45
enzyme immunoassay, 78, 80
eosin methylene-blue agar, 73
EPEC. *See* enteropathogenic *E. coli*
EPEC adherence factor (EAF) plasmid, 68

epidemic curve, 40–41
Epidemic Intelligence Service (EIS), 9
epidemiology, 44–61. *See also* surveillance systems
Escherich, Theodor, 16–20
ETEC. *See* enterotoxigenic *E. coli*
Eubacteria, 18
eukaryotes, 18, 19
evolution of *E. coli*, 65, 98

facultative anaerobe, 20
farm animals, *E. coli* in, 12–14, 37–39, 41, 82, 84, 87–90. *See also* cattle
farm-to-table prevention strategy, 84
fecal-oral transmission, 40, 42, 43
fecal shedding, of *E. coli*, in cattle, 37, 88, 89
fermentation, 73–75
fimbriae, 63, 64, 70
flagella, of *E. coli*, 24, 25, 63
flagellar antigens, 75–76
Food and Safety Inspection Service, 85
foodborne diseases, 20, 46–51, 84–87, 93, 99
FoodNet, 46–49, 54
food preparation, 91–92
food safety guidelines, 47, 91–92, 94
Food Safety Mobile, 94
food supply, 8–11, 14, 38, 39, 43, 53, 84, 85–87
Frobenius, Wilhelm, 16
frozen foods, safety guidelines for, 93
Fungae, 18

gastroenteritis, from ETEC, 31–32
gastrointestinal (GI) tract, enteric bacteria in, 20
gene mutation, in antibiotic resistance, 82
genetic material, in unicellular organisms, 18, 19
genotypes, 31, 32, 33, 72, 75–76, 78–79
Germany, EHEC incidence rate in, 53

GI trots, 31–32
Gram, Christian, 22
gram-negative bacteria, 22–23
gram-positive bacteria, 22–23
Gram stain, 22–23
Graunt, John, 45
ground beef, 8–11, 38, 85–86, 92

H5N1 (avian influenza A), 6
hamburger. *See* ground beef
H-antigens, 75–76
Healthy People 2010, 47
heat-labile enterotoxin, 68
heat-stable enterotoxin, 68
hemolytic uremic syndrome (HUS), 10, 14, 26, 31, 54–56, 67, 81, 98
hemorrhagic colitis, from *E. coli* O157:H7, 31
Hippocrates, 45
historical pathogens, 26
HIV (human immunodeficiency virus), EAEC infections and, 33
hospitalization, for pyelonephritis, 60
host risk factors, 45
Hudson Foods Company, 86
human epithelial cell (HEp)-2 adherence assays, 77–78
humans, 35–37, 38–39, 41, 42, 96, 97
HUS. *See* hemolytic uremic syndrome

Immodium, 83
indole, 75
infectious disease, 26, 27, 29, 44–45, 51. *See also* foodborne diseases
infectious dose, 40
inspection, of meat, 85, 94
International Food Safety Council, 94
intimate attachment, 65–67, 68
intimin, 65, 68

Jack in the Box restaurants, 10–11, 51
Jenner, Edward, 44
juice, *E. coli* outbreak from, 11–12

K-antigens, 64
kingdoms, 18
Klebsiella bacteria, 20
Koch, Robert, 16–17

Lactobacilli, 88, 89
lactoferrin, 97
LEE (locus of enterocyte effacement)
    pathogenicity island, 65, 68
leukocytes, in diagnosing UPEC,
    79–80
lipopolysaccharides, 23, 25, 63–64
Listeria infections, frequency of, 48
livestock, *E. coli* in, 12–14, 37–39, 41.
    See also cattle
livestock inspection, 85
locus of enterocyte effacement (LEE)
    pathogenicity island, 65, 68
loperamide, 83

MacConkey agar, 73, 76
malaria, anti-infective drugs for, 7
Marburg hemorrhagic fever, 6
McDonald's restaurants, 8–10
MDCH-BOL (Michigan Department
    of Community Health Bureau of
    Laboratories), 74
measles, vaccination against, 7
meat, 8–11, 38, 85–86, 91–92, 94, 97
meningitis, 33, 34, 43, 81
methyl violet dye, 22
Michigan, *E. coli* outbreak in, 8
Michigan Department of Community
    Health Bureau of Laboratories
    (MDCH-BOL), 74
Midwest United States, *E. coli* outbreak
    in, 10
misclassification bias, 54
Monod, Jacques, 16
Monster Burger, 10
Montezuma's revenge, 31–32
mucosal membranes, colonization of,
    63
multidrug resistance, 82

National Food Safety Education
    month, 94
natural selection, 65, 98
newborns, 34, 43, 60–61
non-O157 EHEC bacteria, 31, 37, 53,
    75, 78, 79
non-O157 STEC bacteria, 31
normal flora, 35–36, 43
nosocomial UTIs, 59

O-antigens, 63, 75–76, 77
opportunistic infections, from *E. coli,* 34
Oregon, *E. coli* outbreak in, 8
organic compost, *E. coli* contamination
    by, 39
outbreaks, 8–15
    from apple juice and cider, 11–12
    detection of, 51
    from hamburger, 8–11
    from petting farms, 12–14
    prevention of, 84–94
    from radish sprouts, 11
    from water, 14
    by year and location, 13
outer membrane, 23, 25

pandemics, of emerging infections, 6
parasitic infections, anti-infective
    drugs for, 7
Partnership for Food Safety Education,
    90
passive surveillance systems, 46
pasteurization, 11–12
pathogen, 16, 26, 44–45
pathogenesis, 62–71
    of DAEC, 66, 70
    definition of, 62
    of *E. coli,* 62–71
    of EAEC, 66
    of EHEC, 65–67
    of EIEC, 66, 69
    of EPEC, 66, 67–68
    of ETEC, 66, 68
    of UPEC, 70–71

pathogenic *E. coli,* colonization of, 36–37
pathogenicity islands, 65
pathogen risk factors, 45
PCR (polymerase chain reaction), 78–79
Pennsylvania, *E. coli* outbreak in, 12
peptidoglycan, 23, 25
Pepto-Bismol, 83
periplasmic gel, 23, 25
petting farms, 12–14, 41
PFGE (pulsed-field gel electrophoresis), 50–51, 55
phenotype, in diagnosing *E. coli,* 72, 78
phospholipids, 23, 25
phylogenetic lineage, 67
pili (pilus), 63, 67–68
plague, 26
Plantae, 18
plasmids, 65, 69, 82
pneumococcal pneumonia, anti-infective drugs for, 7
pneumonia, from *E. coli,* 34
point source infection, 40–41
polio, eradication of, 7
polymerase chain reaction (PCR), 78–79
polysaccharide, 30
potato vaccine, 95–96
poverty, 28–30
prevention, 84–94, 99
    in agriculture industry, 87–94
    consumer practices, 94
    education in, 90
    in food supply, 85–87
    in meat consumption, 91–92
probiotics, 88, 89
produce, *E. coli* outbreak from, 11, 14, 39
prokaryotes, 16, 19
Protista, 18
pulsed-field gel electrophoresis (PFGE), 50–51, 55
PulseNet, 51
pyelonephritis, 33, 43, 71

radish sprouts, *E. coli* outbreak from, 11
recalls, 85–86
re-emerging infections, 6
reference laboratories, 72–73, 74
refrigeration, 93
rehydration therapy, 83
reservoirs, 12, 37, 42. *See also* cattle
restriction enzyme, 50
risk factors
    for *E. coli* sepsis, 61
    for EAEC infections, 58–59
    for EHEC infection, 53
    for EIEC infections, 58–59
    for EPEC infections, 56
    for ETEC infections, 57
    for hemolytic uremic syndrome, 54–55
    for infectious diseases, 45
    for UPEC infections, 60
    for UTIs, 60

Sakai City, Japan, *E. coli* outbreak in, 11
Salmonella bacteria, 20, 48
SARS (severe acute respiratory syndrome), 6
secondary transmission, 40–41, 42
sepsis, 34, 43, 60–61
serotype, 30, 63–64, 75–76, 77
severe acute respiratory syndrome (SARS), 6
sexual transmission, of uropathogenic *E. coli,* 43
Shiga toxin
    antibiotic treatment and, 81
    antimicrobial treatments for, 98
    in EHEC, 31, 67
        in cattle, 37
        in diagnosis, 78, 79, 80
    as risk factor, 45
Shiga toxin-producing *E. coli* (STEC), 31, 52
Shigella bacteria, 20, 48

siderophores, 70–71

SMAC (sorbitol MacConkey agar), 73–74

smallpox, 7, 26, 44

Snow, John, 45

sorbitol, 73–75

sorbitol MacConkey agar (SMAC), 73–74

spinach, 14, 39

spot indole test, 75

STEC (Shiga toxin-producing *E. coli*), 31, 52

surveillance systems
  for DAEC infections, 59
  for *E. coli* infections in newborns, 60–61
  for EAEC infections, 58–59
  for EHEC infections, 51–54
  for EIEC infections, 58–59
  for EPEC infections, 56–57
  in epidemiology, 46
  for ETEC infections, 57
  for foodborne diseases, 46–49
  for hemolytic uremic syndrome, 54–56
  for UPEC infections, 59–60

swimming, in contaminated water, 14

symptoms, 72

Synsorb-Pk, 98

syphilis, as historical pathogen, 26

thrombotic thrombocytopenic purpura (TTP), 31

transmission, of *E. coli*
  cycle of, 42
  of diarrheagenic *E. coli,* 39–41
  fecal-oral route, 40
  foodborne, 39
  livestock in, 38–39, 41
  to newborns, 43
  person-to-person, 40
  to pregnant women, 43
  secondary, 40–41, 42
  sexual transmission, 43

uropathogenic *E. coli*, 43
  waterborne, 39–40
  zoonotic, 39, 43

traveler's diarrhea, 31–32, 57

treatment, 81–83

Treponema pallidum, 26

TTP (thrombotic thrombocytopenic purpura), 31

tuberculosis, anti-infective drugs for, 7

Turista, 31–32

Umpqua Indian Foods, 85–86

United States
  bioterrorism preparedness in, 98
  diarrheal disease in, 27
  E. coli infection incidence rates in, 53
  EIEC outbreaks in, 58
  foodborne disease outbreaks in, 49
  Healthy People 2010 program of, 47
  poverty in, 30

UPEC. *See* uropathogenic *E. coli*

urinary tract infections (UTIs), 33, 43, 59–60

uropathogenic *E. coli* (UPEC), 15, 33
  antibiotic resistance of, 82
  colonization of, 36
  DAEC and, 70
  diagnosing, 79–81
  incidence rate of, 59–60
  pathogenesis of, 70–71
  risk factors for, 60
  surveillance systems for, 59–60
  transmission of, 43
  treatment of, 81

U.S. Department of Agriculture, 84, 86

UTIs. *See* urinary tract infections

vaccines, 6–7, 88, 95, 97

vacuole, 69

variola virus, 26

vCJD (Creutzfeldt-Jakob disease, human variant), 6
Vibrio infections, 48
viral diseases, anti-infective drugs for, 7
virulence, 63
virulence factors, 62, 63, 65–69, 70–71, 98. *See also* pathogenesis
virulence genes, 62, 64–65, 69
virulence gene screening, 78–79
viruses, 6, 67, 88–89

water, 14, 38–40, 45, 90–94
waterparks, 14
WHO. *See* World Health Organization
women, UTI incidence in, 59–60
World Health Organization (WHO), 9, 83

Yersinia pestis, 26, 48

zoonotic transmission, 39, 43

About the Author

Shannon Manning grew up in Northville, Michigan. She obtained a B.S. in Biology at the University of Michigan, Ann Arbor in 1993. Afterwards she pursued a MPH in hospital and molecular epidemiology with a concentration in public health genetics, and a PhD in epidemiologic science at the University of Michigan School of Public Health. Dr. Manning worked on various research projects involving uropathogenic *E. coli* and group B streptococcus, and completed her graduate work in 2001. In 2002, she was awarded an emerging infectious diseases (EID) research fellowship through the Centers for Disease Control and Prevention (CDC) and the Association of Public Health Laboratories (APHL) where she was placed at the Michigan Department of Community Health, Bureau of Laboratories in Lansing, Michigan. Her primary research projects focused on shiga-like toxin producing *E. coli* (e.g., *E. coli* O157:H7) and *Neisseria meningitidis*.

Dr. Manning is currently employed as an assistant professor at Michigan State University (MSU) in the National Food Safety and Toxicology Center and Department of Pediatrics and Human Development. Her current work involves the molecular characterization of EHEC and group B streptococcus in an attempt to identify genotypes and bacterial factors important for disease pathogenesis. She lives in Howell, Michigan with her husband and four young children.

About the Consulting Editor

Hilary Babcock, M.D., M.P.H., is an assistant professor of medicine at Washington University School of Medicine and the Medical Director of Occupational Health for Barnes-Jewish Hospital and St. Louis Children's Hospital. She received her undergraduate degree from Brown University and her M.D. from the University of Texas Southwestern Medical Center at Dallas. After completing her residency, chief residency, and Infectious Disease fellowship at Barnes-Jewish Hospital, she joined the faculty of the Infectious Disease division. She completed an M.P.H. in Public Health from St. Louis University School of Public Health in 2006. She has lectured, taught, and written extensively about infectious diseases, their treatment, and their prevention. She is a member of numerous medical associations and is board certified in infectious disease. She lives in St. Louis, Missouri.